HOW TO MOBILIZE CHURCH VOLUNTEERS

Marlene Wilson

AUGSBURG Publishing House • Minneapolis

HOW TO MOBILIZE CHURCH VOLUNTEERS

Library of Congress Catalog Card No. 83-70506
International Standard Book No. 0-8066-2012-9

Scripture quotations unless otherwise noted are from the
Revised Standard Version of the Bible, copyright 1946, 1952,
and 1971 by the Division of Christian Education of the
National Council of Churches.

MANUFACTURED IN THE UNITED STATES OF AMERICA

97   16   17   18   19   20   21   22

HOW TO MOBILIZE CHURCH VOLUNTEERS

Contents

Preface

Why does someone write a book? I'm often asked that, and I can only answer for myself. I write a book when I can no longer *not* write it. In other words, when I have thought about the topic, worried over it, explored ideas, read reams of material, and practiced my theories long enough that things begin to come together for me in a meaningful, integrated way, and I experience an overwhelming need to share this information with others, *then* I write a book. I cannot imagine writing about anything I did not care passionately about!

I love the church and care deeply about the problems it faces today. Most major, mainline denominations are experiencing serious membership losses, and most of them don't know why. The vast majority of congregations and parishes are experiencing "the ministry of a handful" in which a small core of members are doing almost all of the work while the rest come to watch on Sunday. This is troublesome organizationally as that handful tends to "burn out" while coming to resent the pew-sitters for their uninvolvement and seeming lack of interest and commitment. But it is much deeper than an organizational problem—it violates our theology! Basic Christian theology relating to the priesthood of *all* believers and the whole body of Christ is being ignored every week in church and after church. It is my belief that this is done not by design, but by default. This book addresses this problem directly and honestly.

One of the clearest directives given to Christians is to "be doers of the word, and not hearers only" (James 1:22). That most certainly does not mean that we simply are all to be active in our congregations or parishes. We are called to minister in our vocations and occupations, our communities, and the world as well. The church does not exist to be served but to provide and equip servants. As someone once said, "It is to be a launching pad, not a hangar." Therefore, the thrust of this book is to help free up the total membership—all of the ministers (99 percent of whom are unpaid)—so that the church may come alive both when it gathers and when it scatters to do its work. My intention is to help the church answer the call sounded by Elizabeth O'Connor in *Journey Inward, Journey Outward* (Harper and Row, 1975):

> Above and beneath and through all calls sounded in our congregation is the call to build the church, to build a community in which people are free to discover who they are, free to discover who others are, and free to discover who God is (page 172).

Acknowledgments

How do I begin to say thank you to the many people who have helped this book become a reality? Perhaps I can at least let you know who they are.

First, I am deeply grateful to two people who have been behind-the-scenes partners in this whole venture (I was about to say silent partners, but they are almost never that!)—Marianne Wilkinson and Warren Salveson. There is so much of them in this book; we spent hours sharing, dreaming, agonizing, laughing, crying, and rejoicing together. I lovingly dedicate this book to them.

Many others helped as well. The Division for Life and Mission in the Congregation of the American Lutheran Church enabled a series of congregational training events in "Volunteerism in the Church" that was the testing ground for much of this material. The participants in those workshops and the many others I've done for interdenominational groups the past four years have provided honest input and evaluation that have kept me out of ivory towers and in the real world. Friends and colleagues have graciously read and critiqued the manuscript and offered invaluable suggestions. Augsburg Publishing House deserves my special gratitude for seeing the need for this book and making it available to you.

As always, I end with a special word of thanks to my dear family. To my mom and dad for raising me, not only in their loving family, but in the church family as well. To Harvey, Rich, and Lisa I am deeply indebted. No one could have a more loving, supportive, and enabling cheering section. They are a part of all I do. Thank you!

Chapter 1

Why Be Involved?
The Theology

On a visit to the supermarket, as I walked down the aisle where dried fruit was displayed, I was struck by a startling thought. The dried prunes, apricots, and pears all neatly packaged in cellophane bags sitting in a row on a shelf reminded me of many of our churches today. The message over that shelf could well have read: "Take some. You may not like us, but we're good for you." So—dutifully— some people chew the prunes. In the same way—dutifully—some people become involved in church activities.

Somehow I cannot believe that is what the church was meant to be. As I read the Gospels, I see other images:

- Salt that seasons the stew.
- Yeast that leavens the loaf.
- Wildflowers showering color on a drab hillside.
- Clear sparkling mountain streams singing on their way, rushing water to a thirsty land.
- A quiet touching of two human beings searching for meaning in a world gone mad.
- Reverent prayer in the midst of the clanging machinery of a modern city.
- A caring word in an uncaring world.

• Searchers coming together to love, strengthen, and enable one another as they eagerly celebrate Word and sacrament together so they can go out and be the church in their daily places.

Part of the dilemma is numbers. As our population has grown, so has the size of our towns, cities, and churches. With greater numbers has come the need to organize, in order to get necessary things done. But too often in the process the verb *organize* has become a noun, and we have become an *organization*. That's where we have lost the theology of it all. The church has found itself just one of many organizations making claims on people's time and lives. And it is not doing too well in that competition because, as "just another organization," it does not stack up very well. It often wastes people's time, uses some people up, uses others not at all, and has vague plans and goals.

So when we talk about learning how to mobilize the people in our churches, it is essential that we pause before getting into the "how-tos" and deal seriously with the "whys." That's really what theology is—the why behind our beliefs and actions. And that is exactly where the church *is* and *must be* different from any other organization. We must be clear about our reasons for both being and doing, or church work becomes just another activity to squeeze in (if we must) or get out of (if we can).

Oscar Feucht in *Everyone a Minister* suggests that the church is an organism—a living, changing, dynamic body—rather than an organization.[1] The reason Christians come together as that body is to receive the power of the Spirit promised to us, not that we might be just an effective organization, but that we might be the *church*. And not the church stacked neatly in a row on every other block in towns and cities, but the church in the everyday lives of real people along the highways and byways of life. That brings us back again to that word *theology*—the why of Christian involvement.

For most people, the term *theology* conjures up images of ancient monks hovering over musty manuscripts and scratching out their wisdom with quill pens. Theology was something the early church leaders worried about, argued over, and finally settled. People divided themselves into denominations that aligned with varying con-

12

clusions about theology—each quite sure they were the possessors of the real truth.

Thus we arrive at today. The monks have changed into professors at seminaries and the pens have become ballpoints, but people still are arguing over, worrying about, and trying to settle this business of theology. And unfortunately the term still has a foreign, musty, awesome, and uninteresting ring to it for most church members.

I would suggest that it's time we take theology out of the hallowed halls, blow off the dust, and bring it into our living rooms, board rooms, and even bedrooms. For theology is not something you merely study—it's something you live!

Perhaps we need some other images of theology. How about:

• steel girders underpinning our actions?
• the skeleton holding our beliefs together?
• the springboard that sends us out into life as unique persons of God?

A person's theology is meant to be personal, vibrant, and ever-growing, not static, impersonal, and boring. It's the stuff of life—beliefs impacting life impacting faith impacting actions impacting beliefs—with God directing the scenario for each of us.

William Stringfellow, in his book *A Public and a Private Faith,* complains about the "academizing of theology." He states:

> One would think that theology is an origination of seminary professors and a possession of only those who are seminary-instructed . . . yet the work of theology is a work of the whole people of God —laity as well as clergy. . . . Theology is quantitatively different from other academic disciplines because it is never an abstract theoretical or just historical exercise, but rather an examination of the actual data of the world's existence in the faith that the Word of God is evident in that data and may be identified, discussed, studied, verified, imparted, and enjoyed . . . theology is a confessional event.[2]

The person who first helped me get a grasp on this business of theology being something you live was Warren Salveson, a Lutheran pastor. He read my first book, *The Effective Management of Volunteer Programs,*[3] which was written for a secular audience and therefore contained no church language or "God words" at all. Warren's reaction to the book, however, was "I want to meet that lady—I like her theology!" and he traveled halfway across the country to attend a seminar I was conducting. When he told me this, it was the greatest compliment of my life. I feel that my philosophy of management and my theology are closely intertwined, and Warren's reaction reinforced that feeling. I felt *congruent*—my words and actions matched! That is what theology is: beliefs being lived out wherever we are.

One of the reasons the average church member has the mistaken notion that theology is only for scholars is that too often the scholars have been so busy discoursing with one another that they have forgotten their role as translators of truth into everyday language and situations. That's why Christ used parables, so every person could understand and lay claim to his truths—farmers, fishermen, business people, homemakers.

Someone once said that making the simple profound is not creative, but making the profound simple is. Christ was truly creative!

This brings us to the question at hand—is there a theology of Christian involvement? If so, what is it? Can we find biblical girders or skeletal support for a Christian's activities in and on behalf of his or her congregation or parish? Let us search the Scriptures:

> But you are a chosen race, a royal priesthood, a holy nation, God's own people, that you may declare the wonderful deeds of him who called you out of darkness into his marvelous light.
>
> 1 Peter 2:9 RSV

> Just as a human body, though it is made up of many parts, is a single unit because all these parts, though many, make one body, so it is with Christ.
>
> 1 Corinthians 12:12 JB

> So we, though many, are one body in Christ, and individually members of one another.
>
> Romans 12:5 RSV

> Each one, as a good manager of God's different gifts, must use for the good of others the special gift he has received from God.
>
> 1 Peter 4:10 TEV

> Now there are varieties of gifts, but the same Spirit; and there are varieties of service, but the same Lord.
>
> 1 Corinthians 12:4-5 RSV

14

Having gifts that differ according to the grace given to us, let us use them: if prophecy, in proportion to our faith; if service, in our serving; he who teaches, in his teaching; he who exhorts, in his exhortation; he who contributes, in liberality; he who does acts of mercy, with cheerfulness.

Romans 12:6-8 RSV

But be doers of the word, and not hearers only.

James 1:22 RSV

But because you are lukewarm, neither hot nor cold, I am going to spit you out of my mouth!

Revelation 3:16 TEV

The evidence seems abundantly clear. We have been created, called, and equipped to be God's people and are therefore expected to act accordingly. These and other passages form the cornerstone of our theology relating to Christian involvement:

• A *theology of gifts*. We each have been created with unique and valuable gifts meant to be discovered, developed, and used on behalf of others. As Oscar Feucht declares, "The individual Christian has a mission in the world no one else can perform for him [her]. It is untransferrable." [4] We each have something of value to give.

• A *theology of the priesthood of all believers*. Christ has declared that *all* believers constitute this royal priesthood. From the earliest tradition of the Old Testament, some of the priests have been called out (ordained) to perform certain special functions such as administering the sacraments and preaching the Word, but 99 percent of the priesthood is unordained laity. Ministry is the work of the whole priesthood, and it involves being called by the Holy Spirit to do six things: proclaim, teach, worship, love, witness, and serve.[5]

I am reminded of a story about a teenage boy who was preparing to teach his first Sunday school class—a group of four and five year olds. When his mother asked him what he was planning to teach at the first class session, he replied, "Well, the lesson plan says to show them that each person is valuable for his or her unique capabilities, and that there is value in differences as well as in

15

conformity . . . *(pause)* and if that doesn't work, I guess we'll make clay bunnies."

I suspect we are all tempted, when faced with that particular lesson plan, to "make clay bunnies," or clean a closet, mow a lawn, go play tennis, or do anything that will keep us from looking seriously at what that heady statement implies. For if we really believe that we, as persons, are unique and important, then it opens up all kinds of questions, possibilities, and responsibilities.

Elizabeth O'Connor, in her book *Search for Silence,* states it well.

> There are all kinds of anxiety in having to leave the land one knows and to be on one's way toward a strange land. No wonder Jesus comments so often on the people who look and look, but see nothing: and hear and hear, but do not understand. If we really saw and heard, we might turn to him and become involved with a migrant people who may have no place to lay their heads when night comes.[6]

That is precisely what we are to do. Keith Miller states:

> The Christian life is a pilgrimage not a program . . . a pilgrimage with people who want to be willing to love, live, and possibly die for Christ, each other, and the world. But they are unwilling to follow any leader who is not ready to be vulnerable to the world and risk it with them. This Christian pilgrimage is a joint adventure, but, to last, it must always remain an individual one to each of us.[7]

The mandate seems clear. We are to be the people of God—a priesthood of all believers—intentionally involving ourselves in ongoing acts of creative love, in God's name, in our homes, in our congregations, in the world. "The church is not an agency to be served, but a work force to be deployed." [8]

Are we acting upon this mandate? Let me share the observations of some respected authorities.

> I see the Christian church in this land opting more for death than life. Most denominations simply are not hard at work to renew the lives of their own members or to reach the unchurched of this land . . . what the church needs is renewal, not reform. The church needs a sense of new birth, an awakening, a more dynamic rela-

tionship to Christ if it is going to have the vitality to do its work and to intersect the drift to the valley of dry bones.

Dr. Lloyd Svendsbye
President
Luther Northwestern Theological Seminary

In most churches the laity belongs chiefly to the audience and is engaged in what we call church housekeeping. Unfortunately the layman's own congregation may have given him this limited image of himself.

Oscar Feucht
Everyone a Minister

At times the churches have regarded themselves as Noah's ark of salvation, fortified camps, God's minorities, spiritual fellowships, ecclesiastical societies, temples where God lives, family clubs, and in many other ways. These half-true notions grow out of the experience of Christians in their environment. Most of these concepts are based on an understanding of the church as a place to go or an organization to belong to. These are "come structures" in contrast to "go structures."

Albert McClellan
*The New Times: A Prophetic Look
at the Challenge to the
Christian Church in the 1970s*

If any or all of those observations are correct, then obviously the church has fallen short of the mark. We can do any number of things about that: (1) become defensive and argue the positive counter-side of the case, (2) feel depressed and mumble "Oh my, ain't it awful!", or (3) take the positive outlook of a quadriplegic friend of mine who said, "I have all the parts—I just need to be rewired." We in the church also have been assured that all the parts are there, so why don't we just get on about the business of some organizational rewiring to enable us to become a fully functioning body?

It is important that we learn how to come together in more loving, caring, and enabling ways as the *gathered church* (within our congregations/parishes) so that we might be equipped to go out as a strong and committed *scattered church*. As Mark Gibbs states:

We are asking for laity who are committed to God's will as revealed in Jesus Christ, and to that will not only on Sunday and in our

17

private religion, not only in church affairs, but also in the whole spectrum of our lives' activities . . . we have to be concerned with Monday's ministries," not only in our personal lives but also in politics and business and industry and commerce. And also in "Saturday's ministries," our involvement in entertainment, in sports, in leisure, in television, in tourism and vacations. And this commitment is to inform all our lives, regardless of our ability or our age, or our sex, or our education, or our race, or our class, or our income, *or our ordination.* Such is the commitment which I believe the New Testament calls us to. And it is for all of us."

What is our possibility of success in this seemingly overwhelming task?

Elton Trueblood says, "The fellowship of weak and unworthy men [and women] can eventually be world shaking, provided it is centered in the life of Christ." Our manual of work must once again be the book of Acts, where we are clearly instructed in how that early handful of ordinary people were able to do extraordinary things.

J. B. Phillips, in introducing his translation of the book of Acts, says this:

These men did not make acts of faith, they believed; did not say prayers, they really prayed. They didn't hold conferences on psychosomatic medicine, they simply healed the sick. . . . But if they were uncomplicated by modern standards we have ruefully to admit that they were open on the God-ward side in a way that is almost unknown today. Consequently it is a matter of sober history that never before have any small body of ordinary people so moved the world that their enemies could say that these men, "have turned the world upside down." [10]

We can take comfort in the promises of Scripture such as Hebrews 4:14-16:

Since then we have a great high priest who has passed through the heavens, Jesus, the Son of God, let us hold fast our confession. For we have not a high priest who is unable to sympathize with our weaknesses, but one who in every respect has been tempted as we are, yet without sin. Let us then *with confidence* draw near to the throne of grace, that we may receive mercy and find grace to help in time of need (italics mine).

18

This is the promise of prayer—the coming of the springtime of the church, when every man [woman] shall know that what he does matters, when every man shall take up the task of making a new life and a new world, when every man shall know that he does not struggle alone.[11]

Notes

1. Oscar Feucht, *Everyone a Minister*, Concordia, 1976, p. 83.
2. William Stringfellow, *A Public and a Private Faith*, Eerdmans, 1962.
3. Marlene Wilson, *The Effective Management of Volunteer Programs*, Volunteer Management Associates, 1976.
4. Feucht, p. 83.
5. Feucht, p. 88.
6. Elizabeth O'Connor, *Search for Silence*, Word, 1972, p. 33.
7. Keith Miller, *Second Touch*, Word, 1967, p. 125.
8. Feucht, p. 106.
9. Mark Gibbs, "The Development of a Strong and Committed Laity," *Laos in Ministry*, April 1982.
10. J. B. Phillips, *The Young Church in Action*, Macmillan, 1955, p. vii.
11. O'Connor, p. 102.

Chapter 2

What Is Happening Now?
The Reality

As we saw in Chapter 1, today's church too often is a happening that never quite happened or, as Thielecke expressed it, dynamite that failed to go off. The pews are filled with potential unrealized and energy untapped. As a result, both the gathered and scattered ministry of the laity is in trouble in a great many churches.

A phenomenon that I describe as "the pillars" and "the pew-sitters" has gradually developed. A faithful core of people do almost everything in the congregation while the vast majority simply observe. Unfortunately, the pillars are burning out (some even change churches and "go underground" to protect themselves) while many pew-sitters are leaving in disaffection and alienation, feeling unneeded and left out.

This situation has affected not only the quality and quantity of the ministry done within many congregations but also the church's ability to be the scattered church. Clergy members have repeatedly told me that out of necessity they ignore or set aside requests for volunteers to reach out to the community because they cannot afford to take a chance on losing some of the precious pillars they need so desperately. They experience a fair amount of guilt over this hoarding but are stymied as to how to change the situation. During the past several years I have given workshops and seminars for dozens of congregations and church bodies of several denominations, and I have found this problem to be almost universal. It therefore behooves those of us who care about the church to examine the problems honestly and to seek solutions. It is essential if we are to actualize the theology we declare regarding the ministry of all believers.

Let us begin with the gathered church and explore some practical problems that have created this ministry of a handful.

Most volunteer ministry jobs in the church are not clearly defined; job descriptions are almost never written. This has created confusion regarding expectations of time and skills needed, responsibility entailed, and training provided. All too often a verbal request is shrouded in such phrases as "It will take you hardly any time" or "It's really nothing much"—and people discover the reality only after saying yes.

Tradition often squelches new and creative ideas and approaches. This has turned many newcomers into pew-sitters. The phrases "We *always* do that here" or "We *never* do that here" have driven many away. Tradition also has severely limited the variety of service opportunities that most churches offer.

Time and talent sheets have helped officially reject people's gifts every year. These surveys should never be filled out if they are not going to be used. It tells people who are never called on either that their gifts are not needed or that they are of little value. Many pew-sitters have received that message very clearly. (We declare that we believe in equality in the stewardship of time, talents, and money, but I have yet to see offers of gifts of money being overlooked or ignored.)

Clergy and lay leaders alike often are very poor delegators. They have not been taught the administrative skill of sharing work creatively and too often end up *doing* instead of delegating. This hampers the process of "growing" new leaders.

The jobs to be filled often receive more attention than the people filling them. Churches have lists of "slots to fill" and often recruit more on the basis of "taking turns" rather than sharing gifts.

It is often difficult for members to describe:
- what they are good at.

- what they are tired of doing.
- what they don't like to do.
- what they want to learn.
- where they are being led to grow.
- when they need a sabbatical.

The need to examine our internal systems of enabling (or disabling) the laity is critical. Every one of these problems can be corrected if we begin to care as much about people as we do programs and demonstrate it by utilizing sound human resource management.

Elizabeth O' Connor, in her book *Eighth Day of Creation,* states:

> We ask to know the will of God without guessing that His will is written into our very being. We perceive that will when we discern our gifts. Our obedience and surrender to God are a large part our obedience and surrender to our gifts. Because our gifts carry us out into the world and make us participants in life, the uncovering of them is one of the most important tasks confronting any one of us.[1]

We have a tremendous challenge before us to lead our members on a journey of discovering who they are in Christ. We must embark on a quest to uncover the unique, unprecedented, and never-recurring potentialities of *each* member—those with quiet gifts as well as those with obvious talents.

Dietrich Bonhoeffer, in *Life Together,* observes:

> The exclusion of the weak and insignificant, the seemingly useless people from a Christian community may actually mean the exclusion of Christ; the poor brother Christ is knocking at the door.[2]

As we begin to help more and more of our lay ministers not only to discover but to actualize their gifts, I have no doubt whatsoever that the internal needs of the church will be met much more effectively. In the process we also will discover many who are ready to be sent out into ministry in the world, and the challenge there will be to help them feel sent, supported, and enabled in their scattered ministries by a caring congregation.

Frederick K. Wentz, in his book *The Layman's Role Today,* lays out the challenge beautifully:

The church must be a catapult that hurls Christ-bearers into every distant corner of human society . . . we must close the gaps between our Sunday faith and our weekday world . . . and between what the church proclaims as the role of Christian lay persons in the world and what the church does to support that role.[3]

There are four areas we need to examine further if we are seriously interested in understanding and improving our management or stewardship of the time and talents of people:

1. leadership;
2. motivation;
3. climate of the organization;
4. organizational systems.

This chapter will analyze what is creating the problems in each of these areas, and Chapters 3 and 4 will explore solutions. It is critically important to understand the problems before trying to solve them. As someone once observed, an uncreative mind can spot wrong answers; it takes a creative mind to spot wrong questions. Let's be sure we have the right questions!

Leadership

In my opinion, leadership is the crux of the entire problem. Through time and tradition a set of habits, attitudes, and styles of leadership have evolved in most churches that are both troublesome and contrary to sound management and leadership principles. Some of these practices are:

• Chairpersons of committees do all the work instead of enabling committee members.

• Clergy and lay leaders alike fail to delegate because "It's quicker to do it myself," or "No one does it quite like I do," or "I don't want to bother anyone."

• Pillars make all the decisions and then wonder why the pew-sitters aren't excited.

• Leaders are asked to cover several major jobs at once (and to keep them far too long); as a result they become "used up."

• Clergy are reluctant to delegate significant roles to lay leaders in traditional "clergy turf" areas (or feel threatened if they do).

24

• Leaders set unrealistic standards of time commitments (due to all the above) that scare others away.

As I mentioned, these habits have too often become the model we see and find ourselves emulating in congregations. "That's how it's done here"—so we tend to go along. The present crisis in most congregations suggests we need to reexamine all of these habits and attitudes. They are both unhealthy and unproductive.

We must take seriously the fact that the leadership style we choose says some very basic things about our philosophy and theology regarding people and work. Some of the most common styles I have seen leaders use are:

Boss—the maker of all significant decisions.

Expert—the knower of all significant things.

Doer—the doer of all significant things.

Hero Martyr—a doer who has burned out.

Abdicrat—someone who retires without leaving; keeps the title without doing the job.

Enabler—a leader who both meets goals and encourages people to grow by involving, supporting, and training them. This type of leader uses the other leadership styles as appropriate, based on the person, situation, and time frame.

People in my workshops repeatedly tell me that working for and with a boss, expert, or doer all too often is not a good experience. These people tend to focus on programs rather than people and thus frequently overlook or diminish the capabilities and ideas of those they are leading, making them feel unimportant and unneeded. A great many of the pillars utilize one of these three styles without realizing the message they are relating to others. What happens to the people led is poignantly illustrated by this story quoted in Mary Schramm's book *Gifts of Grace:*

> Once a little boy went to school. It was quite a big school, but when the boy found he could go right to his room from the playground outside he was happy, and the school didn't seem quite so big anymore. One morning when the little boy had been in school for awhile, the teacher said, "Today we are going to make a picture."
>
> "Good," thought the little boy. He liked to make pictures. He could make lions and tigers and trains and boats. He took out his crayons

25

and began to draw. But the teacher said, "Wait. It's not time to begin." And she waited until everyone looked ready. "Now," said the teacher, "we are going to make flowers."

"Good," thought the little boy, and he began to make beautiful flowers with his orange and pink and blue crayons. But the teacher said, "Wait." She drew a picture on the blackboard. It was red with a green stem. "There, now you may begin."

The little boy looked at the teacher's flower. He liked his better, but he did not say this. He just turned his paper over and made a flower like the teacher's. It was red with a green stem.

On another day the teacher said, "Today we are going to make something with clay." "Good," thought the little boy. He could make all kinds of things with clay—snakes and snowmen and elephants and mice—and he began to pinch and pull his ball of clay. But again the teacher said, "Wait. I will show you how." And she showed everyone how to make one deep dish. The little boy just rolled his clay in a round ball and made a dish like the teacher's. And pretty soon the little boy learned to wait and to watch and to make things just like the teacher's. And pretty soon he didn't make things of his own anymore.

And then it happened that the little boy and his family moved to another city and the boy had to go to another school. On the very first day he went to school the teacher said, "Today we are going to make a picture." "Good," thought the boy and he waited for the teacher to tell him what to do. But the teacher didn't say anything. She just walked around the room. When she came to the boy she said, "Don't you want to make a picture?"

"Yes," said the boy. "What are we going to make?"

"Well, I don't know until you make it," said the teacher.

"How should I make it?" said the boy.

"Why, any way you like!"

"And any color?"

"Any color," said the teacher. "If everyone made the same thing in the same color, how would I know who made what and which was which?"

26

"I don't know," said the boy, and he began to draw a flower. It was red with a green stem.[1]

Leaders who use the boss, expert, or doer style of leadership too often kill the creativity of those led.

Hero martyrs and abdicrats often have trouble either getting the job done or relating well to those they lead because their focus is on themselves. For this reason they are very difficult to work with and frustration is inevitable for those who try.

It is enablers who people long to work with. These leaders see themselves as being responsible for helping those they lead to discover, develop, and utilize their unique and varied gifts and talents while at the same time meeting group goals. They balance the goal-meeting and people-growing aspects of their jobs by removing blocks and creating a climate where people can do their best. Thank God for these servant/leaders.

In my opinion, our leadership training in seminaries, lay leadership schools, and leadership retreats for youth and adults must begin to deal with the issue of leadership style. We must offer new leadership models for people to consider, and honestly confront old habits and attitudes that are disabling to others. It is essential if we are to bring our theology of the priesthood of all believers into the board rooms, committee meetings, and kitchens of our churches. Our words and our actions must become more congruent. Far too many people feel disenfranchised, ungifted, and unimportant!

Here are several quotations that have been of great significance to me in determining my own philosophy of leadership.

No one wanted to be considered the least. Then Jesus took a towel and a basin and so redefined greatness.

Richard Foster
Celebration of Discipline

As leaders we need to be more like gardeners than manufacturers —we need to grow instead of make people. When you want tomatoes, you plant tomato seeds, carefully choose the right soil and place and take care of them. We don't make tomatoes—we allow them to grow.

Unknown

27

A leader is someone who dreams dreams and has visions; and can communicate those to others in such a way that they say "YES."

Michael Murray

The great illusion of leadership is to think that man can be led out of the desert by someone who has never been there.

Henri Nouwen
The Wounded Healer

The greatest good we can do for others is not just to share our riches with them—but to enable them to discover their own!

Sister Corita

The resounding theme throughout these passages is that people are and must be as important as programs in the eyes of the leader. We must be aware of the tremendous impact we have on those we lead. Whether we enable or disable, encourage or discourage them in the process of getting the important work of the church done is to a large extent determined by the leadership style we utilize.

Motivation

"Citizens, you are all brothers, yet God has framed you differently." These sage words of Plato may perhaps help to explain why a 50-year-old friend of mine has just taken a class in aerobic dancing while a 30-year-old neighbor has decided to learn the art of quilting.

One of the delightful things about life is that people are different, not just in physical appearance, but in abilities, emotional makeup, cultural heritage, and in what they like and do not like to do.

It is fascinating to contemplate the whys of behavior. Why do people choose skiing instead of butterfly catching, reading rather than bridge, or auto mechanics instead of medicine? Why does one volunteer prefer to work with delinquent youngsters and another enjoy routine office tasks?

Motivation often has been compared to a scissor with two blades: one blade is what the situation brings to the person (i.e., existing leadership style, climate of the group, job description, training and support, etc.); the other blade is what the person brings to the situation (i.e., motives, needs, attitudes). It is this second blade we want to examine here, for one of the major causes of problems in utilizing volunteers in churches or anywhere else is that we too often get the right person in the wrong job. Another problem is that we frequently overlook changes occurring in people's personal lives that greatly affect both what they are able to do and are interested in doing at any given time. Let's examine some theories of motivation that may help us understand both of these problems.

The book *Motivation and Organizational Climate* presents the work of researchers David C. McClelland and John W. Atkinson. They identify three distinct motives that affect people's work-related behavior:

1. the need for achievement;
2. the need for power; and
3. the need for affiliation.[5]

They point out that motives start in the head; in other words, how we think determines how we act.

Let's use our imaginations a moment and, utilizing the research of Atkinson and McClelland, visualize a huge reservoir of energy. We'll call that reservoir *motivation*. Then let's draw three valves, or openings, in the reservoir through which energy flows, and those we'll label *power, achievement,* and *affiliation.*

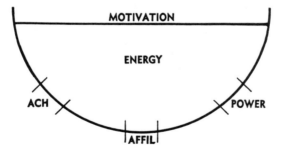

Each motive (the flow through each valve) leads to a different type of behavior. *Everyone has all three valves or motives, but the valves vary as to size and how much they are used from one person to another.*

We might say that a *strong motive* is a valve or energy outlet that opens easily and is larger so more energy can flow through (usually because it's used more). This will determine the type of behavior engaged in by this person.

A *weak motive* is a tight or sticky valve that allows only a tiny bit of energy through—almost like it's rusted shut. Again, this influences types of action or responses on the part of any individual.

McClelland and Atkinson found that the presence and strength of these motives in a person can actually be tested through what is called a *Thematic Apperception Test* (TAT). In this procedure, the individual being tested is shown a set of pictures depicting various social and work situations and is asked to write an imaginative story about each picture. People project their thoughts, feelings, and attitudes into the stories, and the stories provide a sample of what they spend their time thinking and dreaming about. Since how we think determines how we act, this becomes a relatively accurate predictor of behavior.

Obviously we cannot all take TATs or give them to the members of our congregations or church staffs, but we can do the next best thing. By looking at some of the following characteristics and behavior patterns that McClelland and Atkinson have identified with each of the three motives,[6] we can become better able to determine the needs our volunteers and employees bring with them to their jobs. In turn we can create jobs and climates that better meet those needs.

Achievement-motivated people

Goal:

Want to achieve success in situations that require excellent or improved performance.

Characteristics:

- Are concerned with excellence and wanting to do their personal best; set moderate goals and take calculated risks.
- Like to take personal responsibility for finding solutions to problems.
- Have the desire to achieve unique accomplishments.
- Are restless and innovative—take pleasure in striving.

- Want concrete feedback.
- Are better organizers than maintainers.

Spend their time thinking about:
- doing their jobs better;
- accomplishing something unusual or important;
- goals and how they can attain them *and* obstacles and how they can overcome them. (When Sir Isaac Newton was asked how he discovered gravity, he matter-of-factly replied, "By thinking about it all the time!")

Affiliation-motivated people
Goal:
Want to be with others and enjoy mutual friendships.

Characteristics:
- Are concerned with being liked and accepted (interpersonal relationships).
- Need warm and friendly relationships and interaction.
- Are concerned about being separated from other people (definitely are not loners).

Spend time thinking about:
- wanting to be liked and how to achieve this;
- consoling or helping people;
- warm and friendly relationships;
- their feelings and the feelings of others.

Power-motivated people
Goal:
Seek to have impact or influence on others.

Characteristics:
- Are concerned about their reputations or positions and what people think of their power or influence.
- Give advice (sometimes unsolicited).
- Want their ideas to predominate (like Archie Bunker when he said, "It's times like this, Edith, where the only thing holding a marriage together is the husband being big enough to step back and see where his wife is wrong").

- Have strong feelings about status and prestige.
- Have a strong need to influence others, to change other people's behavior.
- Often are verbally fluent, sometimes argumentative.
- Are seen by others as forceful, outspoken, and even hardheaded.

Spend time thinking about:
- how to gain influence and impact over others;
- how to use this influence to win arguments, change people, gain status and authority.

The power-motivation is not a completely negative one, however, McClelland points out some mistaken notions we have in this country concerning the need for power. He states that we have almost totally overlooked the fact that power has two "faces"—one negative and one positive. We tend to assume leaders with power must have dominated their groups and attained their power at the expense of others. This is sometimes true, but not always.

McClelland identifies the negative type of power as *personalized power* and the positive as *socialized power.* He characterizes each as follows: [7]

Personalized (negative)	Socialized (positive)
I win—you lose	I win—you win
Law of the jungle	Exercises power for benefit of others to attain group goals
Prestige supplies (i.e., biggest desk, nicest office, most prestigious title)	Charismatically inspires others to action
Personal power and authority —autocrat	Creates confidence in others— helps them achieve group goals
Makes group dependent and submissive	Makes people feel like origins, not pawns
Exerts personal dominance	An enabler
Tends to treat people like pawns, not origins	

McClelland cautions that if our society insists on overlooking or disregarding the positive use of power, we will continue to see our young people shun public office and positions of leadership. It would seem evident that we must start to reinforce the positive face of power or in the future we will have even more difficulty getting good volunteers to run for positions on church or school boards, city councils, university boards of regents, and city and county planning boards. Like so many other things, power is not bad in and of itself; it is the misuse of it that is bad.

Any healthy organization needs all three kinds of people, for they each do different things well.

Achievers are best at organizing new programs and solving problems. They lose interest when all the kinks have been worked out. They are then ready for a new challenge. They are more goal oriented than task oriented. If you delegate major organizational goals and problems to them, they will happily spend their spare time thinking about them for you and coming up with solutions that work (remember, they do not like to fail).

Affiliators are the nurturers and carers in your midst. They tend to be more task than goal oriented and will enjoy most those tasks that they can do with other people. They are excellent callers (by phone or in person), hosts and hostesses, counselors, greeters, and listeners. They make your church a good place to be.

Power people are the movers and shakers every organization must have to stay in existence. They make the policies, raise the money, negotiate with city hall (and the church hierarchy), and generally hold the body accountable for its actions. In the church, we must realize how much of our mission is related to influencing others: preaching, teaching, stewardship, evangelism. It is important to understand the difference between personal power people (who want positions of influence for their own personal aggrandizement and status and often diminish others in the process) and social power people (who use their power on behalf of others and in the process build the confidence and self-worth of those they lead).

There are needed and suitable jobs for achievers, affiliators, and power people in every congregation, but in most instances no effort is made to match the right person with the right job. Too often the job rather than the person has been the focus.

To illustrate, let me share an experience from one of my church workshops. At a coffee break, after I'd discussed McClelland's theory, two elderly women came up to speak with me. They were extremely excited because they finally understood why one of them had been so miserable the past few months. She identified herself as an affiliator who had been talked into taking over the presidency of the entire women's group of a large church for the next year. She had said yes because it was her turn, and she had been miserable ever since. That day she smiled and told me, "You said it's OK to be an affiliator and that the church needs that too, so I've decided to keep doing what I do best—caring for and supporting others. I don't need to say yes if it doesn't feel right, do I?" She was caught in an all-too-common trap of many organizations—if you live long enough, you'll end up being in charge, ready or not! It was marvelous to see her released from the "oughts and shoulds" of duty and freed for the "may I" of love.

It is important to remember that every group and organization has achievers, affiliators, and power people and that there are jobs to be done that need the special gifts and skills of each. *Matching the right person to the right job is the key*—and we will discuss methods to do this in Chapter 3.

Before we leave McClelland's theory, let me share one other critical area of church life that it helps illuminate. How much of your time is spent in meetings? How often do you leave them frustrated, angry, or just plain "turned off"? Your reaction may have a great deal to do with who was leading the meeting and what type of person you are. Let me explain.

Achievers want short meetings and agendas, quick decisions, very little socializing at meetings, and accomplishing the business at hand as quickly and efficiently as possible. To them, meetings are for reaching decisions and goals.

Affiliators want long meetings, time to share experiences and feelings, loose agendas, lots of coffee and food, and ample socializing opportunities. They see meetings as a chance to get to know one another and build the group.

Can you see how achievers and affiliators can drive one another crazy at meetings? It is important to understand which kind of person you are, and if you are leading meetings, to modify your style a bit to meet some of the needs of everyone and not all the needs of just a few. If you are an achiever, slow the meeting down a bit, have socializing opportunities before, after, or at special meetings, and get more input. If you are an affiliator, tighten up your time and agenda or you will lose all your achievers before the year is out.

34

How varied are our gifts and needs—and how exciting when we begin to see how we need each other to be the fully functioning body of Christ!

Frederick Herzberg further enriches our understanding of motivation by pointing out that it is the work itself that motivates people. He suggests five factors that are motivators: (1) a sense of achievement; (2) challenge; (3) increased responsibility; (4) recognition; and (5) a sense of growth and development.[8] But once again, the many different ways individuals define what they see as challenge or achievement is amazing.

Here is an exercise I have used extensively in groups to illustrate this fact. Have all participants think of the one job they have had (volunteer or paid) that they liked the best and the one they liked the least. As people share their answers, they are surprised to discover that almost everyone's favorite job is someone else's least favorite, and that there is someone who enjoys almost any job (even fund raising, teaching teenagers, bookkeeping, cooking, filing, and long-range planning).

This exercise also is helpful in freeing leaders to be more effective and creative delegators. People can understand why they are reluctant to delegate what they themselves enjoy doing, but they fail to realize how often they hesitate delegating what they dislike doing because they feel guilty about "dumping" it on someone else. What they begin to realize through this exercise is that the tasks they dislike may very well be someone else's favorite thing to do. If they would only become more inventive in sharing their work and in finding ways to invite more people to participate, they would see that there is a right person for every job that needs doing. I am convinced of this based on my seven years of interviewing and placing volunteers in 90 different agencies in our county.

As to the problem of responding appropriately to the life changes that affect our members and how those changes influence their level of involvement, let me share a true story.

A woman who worked at a large church in Colorado as an office manager and administrative assistant loved her job and spent many exciting hours dreaming and planning how to enrich the life of her church. At home, while washing dishes, doing laundry, and making beds, she would explore ideas and mentally play with possibilities.

35

Then she went through a divorce. Suddenly she had no energy or enthusiasm for dreams for her church or job. Instead all her efforts were directed to survival issues—basic needs and concerns such as who would get the children, how she could afford to stay in such a low-paying job, and whether she find an apartment close to the children's school. She had experienced a major life change that affected her energy level, attitudes, needs, and level of involvement.

Similar life changes happen to others all around us, but often we expect them to go on as though nothing has happened. At times our members experience loss of jobs, loss of security, and reduced incomes as well as death, disease, and difficulties in their relationships. Do we allow them the flexibility they need to deal with these changes? Once again, are we in touch with our people as persons with needs as well as with gifts?

Abraham Maslow's well-known theory of the hierarchy of needs may be helpful here. Maslow, a former president of the American Psychological Association, believed that we could learn as much by studying healthy, well-adjusted people as we could by studying those with problems, so that is what he did. His conclusion was that each of us has various levels of need and, as we satisfy one need level, we move up to the next. These needs he categorized as follows:[9]

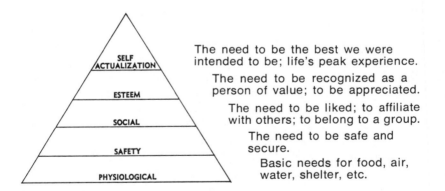

SELF ACTUALIZATION	The need to be the best we were intended to be; life's peak experience.
ESTEEM	The need to be recognized as a person of value; to be appreciated.
SOCIAL	The need to be liked; to affiliate with others; to belong to a group.
SAFETY	The need to be safe and secure.
PHYSIOLOGICAL	Basic needs for food, air, water, shelter, etc.

Maslow made two interesting observations: (1) *Humans are wanting creatures,* and as soon as one level of need is satisfied, we

36

move on to the next. Or, if a basic need suddenly is not met (such as food, shelter, or safety), all other needs become much less important and we regress on the hierarchy. This explains the reactions of the church office worker who was divorced. (2) *A met need is no longer a motivator.*

Do these concepts suggest some interesting possibilities about why people volunteer in the first place? Or choose not to volunteer at all? Or need to change their levels of involvement from time to time?

Finally, no discussion of motivation in the church would be complete without acknowledging that our people come with the most powerful motive of all—faith. Church volunteers are seeking ways to live out what they believe. Scripture repeatedly reminds us to be doers of the Word and not hearers only, to use our God-given gifts and to continually grow in faith and grace. Most of our members long to find places of service (inside or outside the church) to meet these needs. But far too frequently we fail to help them see the jobs and tasks as opportunities for ministry, as ways to put their faith into action. If we ever do learn to do this, my guess is we'll have the church on the move again. It's mind-boggling to contemplate what such an army of believers could accomplish (and if we reread the book of Acts, we'll know!).

Climate

Every organization and subgroup within it has what is called a *climate* or *atmosphere* that determines how it feels to be there. There are friendly climates or stuffy climates, climates that are inviting or foreboding, warm or cold, exciting or dull, cooperative or competitive. The climate of a group is one of the major determinants of whether or not our member volunteers choose to participate, so it is critical for us to understand it if we want fuller participation.

The following two questionnaires will help you assess the climate in your parish and the feelings people have about volunteering there. The questionnaires are most useful when completed by a cross-section of your members. You might use them at a congregational retreat, adult religious educational class, etc.

A Climate Questionnaire

How is the weather in your congregation? Stormy? Sunny? Constantly changing? By thinking of your congregation in terms of a weather metaphor, it is sometimes easier to see more clearly the realities of its *climate,* the combination of factors that sets the tone of an organization and so clearly affects its functioning.

It is important to diagnose the problems of a congregation's climate in order to understand what might need to be changed or improved in it. The following questions can serve to foster fruitful discussions about the nature and needs of the congregation's climate in your parish.

1. What's the weather like around here?

2. How changeable is the weather, and what regular warning signs occur before it changes?

3. How comfortable is it for me here? How comfortable is it for other people with different life-styles or roles? How often do I need to wear foul weather gear?

4. Who are the forecasters on whom we rely to predict what the weather will be like here?

5. Are there different zones within this organization that have very different climates? Who tends to end up in each of these zones?

6. Which people and what types of ideas can grow in this climate? Which die out?

7. Who can do something about the weather here as well as talk about it?

8. Who are the sources of energy in this system? Where are they located?

9. Is there enough breeze (emotional expressiveness) in this system?

10. Is there enough precipitation (conflict and challenge) in this system for people to grow?

Questionnaire adapted from Fritz Steele/Stephen Jenks, *The Feel of the Workplace,* © 1977, Addison-Wesley, Reading, Mass. pp. 177-178. Reprinted with permission.

Volunteers in My Congregation

This exercise is an attempt to get you in touch with the volunteer environment in your congregation. Take a few moments and complete the following sentences. You'll be sharing some of the ideas generated by this exercise.

1. People volunteer to work in our church because:

2. People don't volunteer in our church because:

3. Some things that turn volunteers off in our church are:

4. People feel good about volunteering in our church when:

From "Congregational Workbook," *Volunteerism in the Church* workshops, Division for Life and Mission in the Congregation of the American Lutheran Church, 1980.

According to Litwin and Stringer, there are at least nine factors that greatly affect climate.[10] Let's examine each one briefly, especially as it affects volunteers within churches.

1. *Relationships.* How rigidly defined and separated are the roles of clergy and laity, pillars and pew-sitters? Is there lack of clarity in job definitions, poor delegation, responsibility without authority, a feeling of distrust or threat? Or do all members feel they are part of a synergic team where the whole is greater than any of its parts and they are better together than alone?

2. *Rewards.* How does your congregation say thank you to volunteers, both those involved in the congregation and in the community? Do you reward only the obvious talents, or the quiet gifts as well?

3. *Warmth/support.* Do people feel supported, enabled, and equipped by both clergy and lay leaders to succeed at what you ask them to do? How often do you laugh (and cry) together?

4. *Conflict.* How do you handle conflict—or do you? Conflicts that are denied or ignored often go underground and create a

climate of uneasiness and uncertainty. Is questioning OK, or is conformity the expectation?

5. *Physical setting.* Does your church have a hospitable and inviting climate that makes *everyone* (new or old, active or inactive, clergy or laity) feel welcome and cared for? How antiseptic or lived-in is your house of God?

6. *Identity.* The leadership styles utilized have a tremendous impact on this factor. Do all members feel as if they belong and are valuable children of God, with unique gifts to share? Or does your climate reinforce the ministry of a handful?

7. *Standards.* Has the congregation identified its mission, goals, and objectives? Does each member see himself or herself as an important contributor to both setting and accomplishing these goals and objectives? If the congregation has an exciting sense of mission —of being involved in more than maintenance functions—the climate comes alive and enthusiasm spreads.

8. *Creativity/risk.* How often are the phrases "We always" and "We never" used in your congregation? Must everyone play it safe by acting in accepted, predictable ways due to fear of failure and censure? A climate that nurtures creativity allows for calculated risk and some failure. Without risk there can be no change, and where there is risk there will be some failures. Do you view these creative ventures as opportunities for growth and learning—or as unacceptable deviations?

9. *Congregational expectations.* Are both rules and roles set in concrete in your congregation? Is red tape keeping people from trying out skills and ideas? Do you expect the impossible from your congregational leaders and clergy in the way of their obligations and time commitments?

One comforting fact about organizational climate is that we *can* do something about it. It's different from being stuck with Montana snowstorms, East Coast humidity, or Kansas tornadoes. If we don't like the "weather," we need to change it. Most congregations are pretty healthy and robust in some of those nine factors and pretty weak and puny in others. A careful analysis of the worksheets in this chapter and these nine climate factors can help you know where to begin. Another extremely helpful resource is the book *The Feel of the Work Place* by Fritz Steele and Stephen Jenks (Addison-Wesley, 1977). It is both insightful and practical in recommending ways to change climate. Concrete suggestions and tools to deal with most of the climate problems will be made in later chapters of this book as well.

Organizational systems

At times its seems we have lost sight of the fact that the good news we proclaim to others must first reverberate in the halls of our own committee rooms and council chambers. We too often have become so worn out in getting our "churchy" jobs done that we forget why we are doing them in the first place. To correct this:
- "slots" must become ministries;
- "members" must become unique individuals;
- "oughts and shoulds" must become "may I's" of love;
- "turns" must become opportunities to share gifts.

We need to look with new eyes and open hearts at the theological concepts of "the priesthood of all believers" and "the ministry of the laity," to rediscover them as the priceless treasures they are. As children of God, each one of us is called, equipped, and supported to do the work of God. How can that be boring? But too often we have made it just that.

Often we barely know *what* we are asked to do, so it is easy to understand how we can lose sight of the *why*. Someone needs ten of these (Sunday school teachers), four of those (choir members), seven of these (ushers), etc. Here again the emphasis is on the *slots* needing to be filled rather than on the *persons* filling them.

Of course, none of this has happened intentionally. We simply have forgotten God's promises of gifts and miracles and being called as unique children of God. And we have become sloppy in our management of our human resources. When did your church last have a major "people-raising" event? Yet we have fund-raising events all the time. Unfortunately, our stewardship of money has received far more careful attention than our stewardship of time and talents. Let me explain.

Has someone ever refused to receive a gift you wanted to give?

41

How did you feel? Were you hurt? Angry? Confused? Somehow diminished? We do this in the church all the time—in the systematic rejection process labeled *time and talent sheets*. Here is an all-too-common scenario.

> Jane Whosit was new—still not fully comfortable in or accepted by her new church, St. Johns. Her problem was shyness. How she wished she could overcome it—but that's the way she'd always been. She wanted so much to be a part of things, but she had no idea how to go about it. Then one day a letter came. It was the stewardship form for the year. Deciding about her gift of money was no problem, but she agonized over the time and talent portion. She had time but very little confidence in any talent she had to share. Yet she wanted to give more than just money—it might be the answer to her really becoming a part of this group, known and accepted. She lay awake for hours agonizing over what to check. What if she tried something and failed? What if . . . ? What if . . . ? In the morning she reviewed the list again and finally checked two things: typing in the office and helping with kindergarten in Sunday school. She felt a small thrill of anticipation, for at last she'd have a place to be a part of her church. She laid her form on the altar on Stewardship Sunday and then waited for the phone to ring. She waited . . . and waited . . . and waited. . . .

> Then there's Mrs. Oldstandby—a pillar. She is at present president of the St. John's women's group, on the church council, and sings in the choir. She was just asked to help out in the church office next week while the secretary is on vacation. She said yes because she did not want to let the pastor down and then lay awake all night trying to figure out how she was going to juggle that job on top of everything else.

Of course, no one means to overlook Jane Whosit or burn out Mrs. Oldstandby, but it happens all the time. Churches seem to use people up or miss them altogether. That is the dilemma! It continues because we have not instituted systems to see that it doesn't. The next two chapters are about doing just that.

Notes

1. Elizabeth O'Connor, *Eighth Day of Creation*, Word, 1971, pp. 14-15.
2. Dietrich Bonhoeffer, *Life Together*, Harper and Row, 1954, p. 38.
3. Frederick K. Wentz, *The Layman's Role Today*, Abingdon, 1963, p. 39.
4. Mary R. Schramm, *Gifts of Grace*, Augsburg, 1982, pp. 51-53.
5. George H. Litwin and Robert A. Stringer Jr., *Motivation and Organizational Climate*, Harvard University Press, 1968, p. 8.
6. Litwin and Stringer, pp. 14-24.
7. David McClelland, 'Two Faces of Power," quoted in *Journal of International Affairs*, Columbia University, Vol. 24, No. 1, 1970, pp. 29-47.
8. Litwin and Stringer, p. 8.
9. Paul Hersey and Kenneth H. Blanchard, *Management of Organizational Behavior*, 2nd ed., Prentice-Hall, 1972, p. 26.
10. Litwin and Stringer, pp. 81-82.

Chapter 3

What Can We Do about It?

The Tools

The concept of needing tools to make or repair things is not new to us. Mechanics use tools to fix our cars, cooks use tools (utensils) to cook a meal, carpenters use tools to build a house. One of the ways you can tell if you have found a professional or an expert to do a job is to notice if they come equipped with the appropriate tools. (A plumber who asks if he can borrow your wrench would hardly evoke your confidence.)

Yet in the important business of building up the church to be fully functional and alive, we have neglected to identify or use many of the appropriate tools available to us. We often flounder around believing good intentions and pure motives will make everything come out all right—especially since this is God's work we are about!

Most seminaries have not even acknowledged that these tools are important, nor have they done anything to help our professionals (the clergy they ordain) know how to use them. It's assumed they either already have them or will somehow learn by osmosis on the job. I have had countless pastors of several different denominations confirm this and express how desperately they wish that concepts and tools like those covered in this book had been a required part of their seminary training. They come out well grounded in theology but sorely lacking in management and motivational skills, and that is where congregations are in trouble.

If we are serious about wanting to close the gap between our theology of involvement (Chapter 1) and the reality of today's churches (Chapter 2), we must acquire the tools to help us do it effectively. The tools I am referring to are the tools of management. Because of some of the preconceived notions people have about business and corporations and in light of my earlier comment that the church is an *organism* rather than just another *organization,* I can imagine immediate resistance to this solution. But think about it in comparison with a human body. Nothing more highly organized or intricately coordinated exists in the world. When even the smallest part of that organism fails to function, it affects the entire body. I would maintain the same is true for the church body.

I first began to realize how important sound management is in working with volunteers when I was director of a volunteer center in Boulder, Colorado. We helped recruit, interview, and place volunteers in 90 different health, educational, welfare, and recreational organizations in our county. I held that job for seven years, and during that time I interviewed hundreds of volunteers. One question we always asked them was, "Why did you leave the last place you volunteered?" I was astounded at how frequently the reasons were: "I never knew what they wanted me to do; I didn't even have a job description;" "I didn't know who I was responsible to, so I never knew who to go to with questions, ideas, or problems;" "They never provided any training to help me do what I was asked to do;" "Nobody ever told me if what I was doing was helpful or not;" "I was asked to do more and more and finally just burned out!" These problems occurred because, at that time, many volunteer organizations were not utilizing management tools either—and volunteers fell through the cracks.

During the past decade the field of volunteerism has seriously addressed these problems and enormous strides have been made in correcting them. College courses, books, and workshops all offer sound, practical help in the management of volunteers.

After having been deeply involved in the secular volunteer management field for 15 years, it came as a shock to me to realize how I had been separating my Sunday and weekday worlds. I had seen clearly the need for management skills in secular volunteer groups, but it took a long time until it occurred to me how similar the need was in the church. Church volunteers were leaving in frustration for all the same reasons that volunteers were leaving other organizations. It took them a bit longer to burn out, but when they did they were even more disillusioned because they felt the church should somehow have cared more about them than it apparently did.

What volunteers repeatedly have said they want and need are:

- to be carefully interviewed and appropriately assigned to a meaningful task;
- to receive training and supervision to enable them to do that task well;
- to be involved in planning and evaluating the program in which they participate;
- to receive recognition in a way that is meaningful to them;
- to be regarded as persons of uniqueness;
- to be accepted as a valued member of the team.

All of these needs can be dealt with if we acquire and use the management tools presented in this chapter.

First let us define the term *management*. It simply means working with and through other people to accomplish organizational goals and purposes. Since 99 percent of the church's work force is unpaid and unordained member volunteers, learning how to work "with and through" them is essential.

The functions a manager or leader needs to perform are the same whether he or she is managing IBM, the Red Cross, or St. John's Church. They are: [1]

1. **PLAN** — GOALS / OBJECTIVES
2. **ORGANIZE** — PLANS / JOB DESIGNS
3. **STAFF** — RECRUIT / INTERVIEW / PLACE
4. **DIRECT** — TRAIN / SUPERVISE
5. **CONTROL** — EVALUATE

Another way to envision these functions is in the framework of building a bridge from where we are now to where we want to be, using the various functions of management as the necessary building blocks for the bridge:

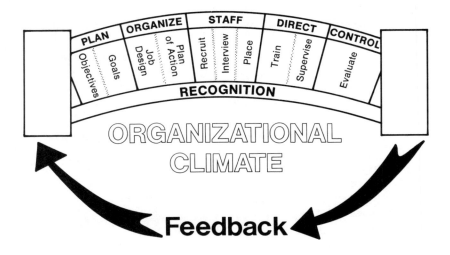

This illustration helps us see clearly how important it is not to leave out any of the blocks and that we must start building at the beginning, rather than in the middle, of the bridge. Many volunteer organizations make the mistake of starting with recruitment rather than planning and end up with people they don't know what to do with—disastrous!

Let's examine each of these functions or building blocks.

Planning

It is important to consider not only *how* to plan effectively, but *who* should be involved in the process. This example shows us why:

> As a pastor, I've never been able to get too excited about somebody else's program. Not even if it comes from the conference president. . . . But when it's *my* program, something opens up within me, and I invest incredible amounts of time and energy to

achieve its success. Why has it taken me so long to see that the members of my church are no different? How many years I've wasted trying to get them to do things they had no desire to do, while practically ignoring the potential of their own hopes and dreams concerning their church and their Lord! . . . I have finally learned that the right question to ask [as pastor] is not: How can we get our members to do what we want them to do? It *is:* How can we help our members fulfill *their own* needs for involvement, commitment, and successful ministry in the church? [2]

This pastor has discovered what studies have proven over and over—people are committed to plans they help make. Yet this frequently is overlooked by both clergy and lay leadership. So, the first principle of good planning is to involve those affected by the plan in the process.

The basic questions you are trying to answer in any planning process are:

- Where are we now (baseline assessment)?
- Where do we want to go (goals and objectives)?
- How will we get there (action plans and strategy)?
- How long will it take (time line)?
- How will we know when we get there (evaluation)?

To answer these questions, it is important to go through three steps in the planning process. Various management experts label these steps differently, so be careful not to get hung up on terminology or word games here. It really does not matter what you call the steps as long as you do all three. Those three steps (in my terminology) are *goals, objectives,* and *action plans.*

1. *Goals.* The broad statement of mission or purpose that defines the *why* of an organization or group is its goal. It is usually global enough to encompass all that is done by that organization (i.e., wipe out poverty; provide educational opportunities for adults; establish and maintain residential care facilities for abused children; etc.) An example of a goal or mission statement for a congregation might be:

The mission of this congregation shall be to glorify God and to help in the extension of God's kingdom by living and sharing the Christian faith as expressed in the doctrine and practice of the church.

49

Most congregations and parishes have such a statement, but few of the members know what it is. It should be shared with everyone, for everything that is done should reflect and further that goal.

One main problem with planning is that many groups stop the process here. Goals are fun to write—they are global and visionary. The difficulty is that goals are unachievable; therefore, no one can hold us accountable for them. We must break down that goal or mission into objectives to make it manageable and able to be done.

2. *Objectives.*   The specific, measurable, achievable steps we intend to take this year to help us move toward meeting our goal are our objectives. How exactly do we plan to share our faith? To whom (what neighborhood, age, or ethnic group) will we reach out? When?

It is when we perfect this skill that we begin to turn dreams and wishes into reality. For example, your church may wish it could involve more single adults in its programs. If you were to turn that wish into an objective, it might look like this: *To survey the needs of all single adults in our congregation by December of this year.*

Or take the constant concern about teenagers leaving the church. How about turning a worry into an objective: *To interview and place 10 teenagers from this congregation in meaningful volunteer ministries based on their interests and career goals by June of next year.*

Then there is the wish on the part of many congregations that they might be able to do something about world hunger (other than just have a day of fasting every so often). An objective might be: *To form an interdenominational food bank on the southwest side of our city by January of next year.*

To illustrate the difference between goals and objectives, let me use an analogy. If you have ever hiked in the mountains, you are familiar with switchbacks. These are short, zigzagging trails that cut across the mountains to help hikers get to the top. The goal, in this case, is to reach the top of the peak. The switchbacks are like objectives—short, manageable, measurable steps to help us get there. Most church planners forget the switchbacks and just try to scale the sheer cliff.

3. *Action plan.*   Every objective must have an action plan that

answers four critical questions: *who, how, when,* and *budget required.* This is the tool that helps your leadership delegate responsibility in a sensible, meaningful fashion.

Check the action plans for the year and see if a handful of pillars are filling most of the significant jobs. If their names appear in all the *who* columns in your plans, you need to change that situation. Write some objectives: *To limit each member to one major leadership role per year. To establish a viable leadership training course for new members by the end of this year.*

Planning is simply a tool, not an end in itself. Use it well, but don't spend all your time on it. As Elizabeth O'Connor states: "To be in earnest about a vision is to think about strategy—how to take what is out in the distance and bring it into the here and now where it can be perceived by ordinary sight." [3]

Organizing

"Recruiting before designing jobs is rather like trying to dance before the music begins. The possibility of ending up out of step is very good indeed." [4]

After a congregation and each department or committee within it has completed its planning for the year, then it is time to organize the work that needs to be done into sensible, feasible jobs (or, as I prefer to call them, *volunteer opportunities*). Earlier in this chapter we learned how frustrated volunteers become when their work is not clearly defined and when they do not have written job descriptions.

It is also important that these volunteer ministry positions are examined each year to make sure they are still meaningful in light of current congregational goals and objectives. Sometimes jobs are perpetuated long beyond their usefulness. As Abraham Maslow warned, "What's not worth doing is not worth doing well." Be sure you are not wasting people's precious time and energy.

That does not mean that jobs do not vary a great deal regarding responsibility and time commitment. Some duties may be less responsible than others (such as mailing out newsletters, typing form letters, etc.), but if it is important that these be done, they are

Description of Volunteer Opportunities

Job title:

Responsible to:

Job description:

Time required:

In-service training provided:

Qualifications and special skills:

Comments:

From *The Effective Management of Volunteer Programs* by Marlene Wilson, Volunteer Management Associates, 1976.

legitimate, and they very likely will suit someone in the congregation perfectly. (See Appendix A on page 125 for a chart describing how jobs of different levels of responsibility should be written).

The format used to define volunteer opportunities should be simple, concise, and include the necessary information. The above form is an example.

Designing work so that it has meaning and provides satisfaction is an art, one that most organizations have not mastered very well. Far too often work is dumped rather than delegated or is in illogical, unsatisfying, perplexing bits and pieces.

Besides writing out the description of the job as just suggested, several other things can be done:

• Overwhelming jobs (like Sunday school superintendent) can be broken down into more manageable segments.

• Boring, repetitive jobs can "grow" or be expanded to include more variety, e.g., the person who files also can set up the filing system, the person who types the newsletter may want to gather news for it as well, etc.

• Two or more small jobs that require two people once a week for one hour may be combined to better utilize the time of one person for two hours.

• Two people may want to share the same job to accommodate today's busy schedules (e.g., two Sunday school teachers may alternate, each teaching a class every other Sunday).

• Jobs can be designed for shorter periods of time for today's working members. The time of open-ended or forever commitments is over. Most working people prefer three- to six-month assignments whenever possible.

• Jobs can be added or changed to utilize the gifts of members (e.g., an art class for seniors could be added when an artist is discovered in your midst; a cartoonist may greatly enliven a vacation Bible school staff; a photographer could create a slide show for the stewardship drive that depicts your congregation in action).

The more creative you are in designing these opportunities, the more people you are apt to interest in becoming involved. Variety is not only the spice of life, but of the church as well.

Staffing

Next comes the most critical, exciting, and difficult part of the whole management system—finding the right person for the right job. Because so many of our problems are the result of getting the right person into the wrong job, the matching process, in my opinion, is the key to success in effectively working with volunteers. There are three components to the staffing process: *recruiting, interviewing,* and *placing.*

Recruiting

Defining jobs well will solve nothing unless you can find members interested in filling them. That is where recruitment comes in. Many churches have adopted what my friend Warren Salveson calls the "Buffalo Bill" method of recruitment. That means riding into a herd of buffalo and, as they scatter, looking for the stray that lags behind because it is not fast or cunning enough to get away—and lassoing it.

We look for those members who haven't learned how to get away, and we snag them into doing what we need done, regardless of whether the job has anything to do with their gifts or interests. Unfortunately, there's a great deal of truth in this observation.

Another method often used is to telephone someone with the pitiful plea that you have asked everyone else you could think of, and this person is your last hope. Have you ever thought what that says to a person about his or her own value and worth? It's hardly affirming or motivating. If you get a yes, it's out of guilt or pity. A Presbyterian minister colleague of mine has observed that "people do not like to be should upon anymore!" He's right. There are several more effective and certainly more caring ways to go about the business of recruiting member volunteers than on the basis of "oughts," "turns," or sheer desperation.

First, there is the intentional recruiting of a particular person for a specific job because he or she has demonstrated the gifts needed. For example, if a member is an achiever who in the past has effectively tackled organizing a new youth group or solved a problem relating to revamping your stewardship drive, you might very well approach that person the next year to head up your new volunteer ministries project (or outreach to singles program, etc.). Appendix B, "A Checklist before Linking a Volunteer," on page 126 offers some guidelines for recruiting this person effectively. Remember to be honest with the person. Allow lead time for the person to think about the job, and be aware of other things going on in his or her life (e.g., a major life change or crisis, another major commitment for the year).

Be prepared to allow the person to say no gracefully. If a person says yes because he or she feels pressured to do so, the commitment you get may be grudging or halfhearted.

However, do not make the assumption that just because a member says no to a specific request, the person does not want to become involved at all. When this happens, very seldom is any follow-up done to see where the individual *would* like to serve. Consequently a suitable referral is not made to another committee or program. This is a grave mistake often made by church leaders that has turned many potential volunteers into pew-sitters. After their first no, they were never asked again. At this point, an ongoing system of follow-up is necessary.

Another type of recruitment is more general. Once volunteer jobs have been designed, you need to let people know what they are so they can let you know what they are interested in doing. This is done through time and talent sheets, church newsletters, bulletin announcements, etc.

In this type of recruitment, however, I do not believe that just anyone who raises a hand or walks through the door should get the job. For years volunteer organizations recruited and placed this way: "If they're warm and breathing and say yes, we've got to take them." Yet if a person is not suited for a job, it is not fair either to the person or the group to place them in it. Certainly we care more about both our mission and our people than to subject them to that system.

Instead, volunteer opportunities should be attractively advertised or displayed so all members are aware of the opportunities for service offered. One idea is to have a rack in your fellowship hall or narthex where all job descriptions are displayed in colorful folders by job type (music, education, work with small children, office, administration, etc.). People can then browse through them and contact the designated person to get more information. This would be especially effective with newer members who are eager to become involved but often do not know where or how. (Appendices C, D, and E on pages 126-131 offer some other suggestions regarding time and talent surveys and follow-up).

Interviewing and placing

After people indicate an interest in a particular type of volunteer ministry, it is essential that someone follow up with them. This is where the interview comes in. An interview is simply a "conversation with a purpose," and the purpose in this case is to allow members to tell someone about their interests, skills, and feelings about involvement. In Chapter 2 we noted that members seldom have a chance to express:

- what they are good at;
- what they are tired of doing;

- what they don't like to do;
- what they want to learn;
- where they are being led to grow; and
- when they need a sabbatical.

An interview with a volunteer ministries coordinator (or other designated person) allows this to happen.

The two essential ingredients of an interview are: (1) asking appropriate, open-ended questions (those that allow the other person to talk about themselves), and (2) active listening. The following is a list of some of the practices of a good listener. Check those you feel you need to work on—at church, work, home and with friends.

1. Listen to understand, not to ready yourself to reply, contradict, or refute. This is an extremely important attitude.

2. Remember that understanding involves more than knowing the dictionary meaning of the words that are used. It involves, among other things, paying attention to the tone of the voice, the facial expressions, and the overall behavior of the speaker.

3. Observe all this and be careful not to interpret too quickly. Look for clues to what the other person is trying to say, putting yourself (as best you can) in the speaker's shoes, seeing the world as the speaker sees it, accepting the speaker's feelings as facts that have to be taken into account—whether you share them or not.

4. Put aside your own views and opinions for the time being. Realize that you cannot listen to yourself inwardly and at the same time listen outwardly to the speaker.

5. Control your impatience. Listening is faster than talking. The average person speaks about 125 words a minute but can listen to about 400 words a minute. The effective listener does not jump ahead of the speaker but gives the person time to tell the story. What the speaker will say next may not be what the listener expects to hear.

6. Do not prepare your answer while you listen. Get the whole message before deciding what to say in return. The last sentence of the speaker may give a new slant to what was said before.

7. Show interest and alertness. This stimulates the speaker and improves performance.

8. Do not interrupt. When you ask questions, it is to secure more information, not to trap or force the speaker into a corner.

9. Expect the speaker's language to differ from yours. Do not quibble about words; try to get at what is meant.

10. Your purpose is the opposite of a debater's. Look for areas of agreement, not for weak spots that you plan to attack and blast with an artillery of counterarguments.

11. Before giving an answer in a particularly difficult discussion, sum up what you understand the other person to have said. If your interpretation is not accepted, clear up the contested points before attempting to proceed with your own views.

Appendix F (page 132) includes a letter with some nondirective questions our congregation developed to be used in one-to-one interviews with members. We selected and trained a group of volunteers to conduct these interviews and sent the letter before the interview session. We found people responded very positively to the opportunity to discuss important matters with a fellow Christian whose only agenda was to get to know them better. Appendix F also includes a worksheet to be used by the interviewer following the visit.

Another method that has been used very effectively is to have a group (such as women's circle, adult Sunday school class, or leadership retreat group) fill out the questionnaire "Discovering My Gifts" on page 58 and discuss it in pairs. It's amazing what we can learn about ourselves and one another!

This business of helping people identify, develop, and use their God-given gifts is vitally important, not just so we can involve more people as volunteers, but for their sakes as well. Elizabeth O'Connor states in *Letters to Scattered Pilgrims,*

> Every inward work requires an outward expression, or it comes to naught . . . this is why a person's work is always of utmost importance. "Being" and "doing" complete each other, as do "staying" and "going." We cannot choose one above the other without falling into great trouble.[5]

Discovering My Gifts

Answer the following questions from the standpoint of the area in your life you currently are most excited about (church, job, home, family, school, social life, leisure time, hobbies, etc.).

1. Some things I believe I do well are:

2. Some things I think I'm not very good at are:

3. If given the chance, I think I *might* be good at:

4. One *new* thing I have tried recently that went pretty well was:

5. Who encouraged me to try the above? What made him or her think I could do that? Does he or she often encourage me to try a new thing?

6. Who are the "mentors" (the wise, loyal advisers) in my life?

And Milton Mayerhoff, in his book *On Caring*, shares this observation:

> Caring must not involve me in a peripheral way only; I must be able to make use of my particular gifts. Unless my distinctive powers are sufficiently called into play, my caring cannot significantly order my life. I am not fully engaged and I feel somewhat denied.[6]

Directing

This function assures that we do not just place people in jobs and then forget about them. It is essential to provide both supervision and training if volunteers are to feel equipped and supported.

Supervision means more than "checking up" on people. It means providing leadership, information, time, and caring. If you will recall, Chapter 2 discussed styles of leadership. (Please review pages 24-28). Your style of leadership will greatly impact both how you train and how you supervise those who work with you. If you are a boss, expert, or doer, you probably will share little of your work or yourself. If you are an enabler, this function of directing and leading becomes your primary focus. Your goal becomes finding out how you can help others succeed in what you have delegated to them. If you are not sure what they need from you, you ask.

The art of communication is involved very clearly in fulfilling both the tasks of supervision and training. Carl Rogers, a noted communications expert, states there are three essential ingredients in effective communication: [7]

1. *Congruence.* We are who we *really* are with one another, with no masks or pretense. (Martin Buber calls this the difference between "being" and "seeming.")

2. *Empathy.* We let the other person know we are truly open to what they are saying *and* feeling.

3. *Positive regard.* We have a genuine, positive regard for the other person *as a person.* Rogers calls this "nonpossessive caring." (Anne Lindbergh once said, "Those I love, I wish to be free—even of me.")

When we have this kind of communication, wonders begin to happen. Suddenly our theology about caring becomes real, and people feel it.

Reuben Gornitzka, in *Who Cares,* reminds us, "We can't simply cheer people on and give them our best wishes. We have to make room for them in our own lives." [8]

Dietrich Bonhoeffer adds this warning, "We must be ready to allow ourselves to be interrupted by God. He will be constantly crossing our paths and cancelling our plans by sending people with claims and petitions." [9]

A story is told about a college professor who used to become very annoyed at all the students who kept interrupting his work. Then one day he came to an amazing realization: those interruptions *were* his work. We need to come to such a realization. The following worksheets and information will help clarify the things you need to keep in mind when training and supporting volunteer workers.

The Training Process

1. Identify expectations. Use job descriptions, persons who have done the job, persons who expect the job to be done.

2. Assess learning needs. Ask persons who have done the job what they needed to know. Find out where the learners are. The gap between what they know and what they need to know is the need.

3. Determine objectives. Decide which of the needs can be dealt with through training. (Systems problems cannot.) Prioritize and select the needs to be dealt with.

4. Develop program content. Decide what skills, knowledge, attitudes the learners need.

5. Design the learning experience. Select methods and materials. Decide what approaches will be effective.

6. Obtain instructional resources. Arrange for persons, media, equipment, materials, and place.

7. Conduct training. Create and maintain a learning environment. Present information. Direct and monitor activities. Plan for and manage individual participation.

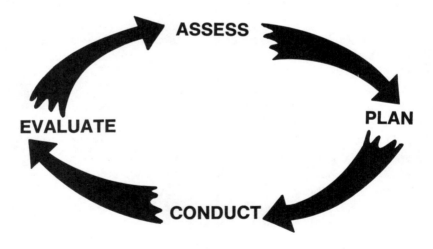

ASSESS

PLAN

EVALUATE

CONDUCT

From "Congregational Workbook," *Volunteerism in the Church* workshops, Division for Life and Mission in the Congregation of the American Lutheran Church, 1980. Developed by Marianne Wilkenson, Hollis Renewal Center, Kansas City, Mo.

Planning Sheet—Training Plan

Who is to be trained?	Major emphasis	Who knows the job?	Resources available	Form of training	Timing methods	Equipment, materials needed

From *Volunteers Today: Feeding, Training, and Working with Them* by Harriet Naylor, Dryden and Assoc., 1967, 1973.

Information Form: Training

This tool is used by the task group on training volunteers. A member of the task group uses the form as a guide for conducting an individual or group interview to secure information which will assist the task group in planning a training program for the congregation.

1. Ministry position_____

2. What would someone beginning this ministry for the first time need to know or need help with in order to do the ministry well?

3. What experiences, training, or resources have been helpful to you as you have done this ministry?

4. What would you want to say to the person who follows you in doing this ministry?

5. What suggestions would you like to make to the task group working on training volunteers?

6. Other comments:

Interviewer_____Date_____

Ways to Support and Recognize Volunteers

Volunteers in churches often are taken for granted. They, and the services they provide, often are unrecognized, unthanked, and unsupported. Yet, they deserve our recognition and gratitude. The role of the volunteer in the life and ministry of the church is an important one. Indeed, the life and ministry of the church depend on those who volunteer their time and effort to do the various tasks and services necessary or helpful for the effective and faithful functioning of the church. Without such volunteers there probably would be no church or ministry or society as we know them today.

Following is a beginning list of ways to support and recognize volunteers and the work they do within the local church, in the wider church, and in the community. Add your own creative ideas and then plan how to implement as many as possible.

• Publish a list of persons who volunteer within the local church, in the wider church, and in the community and distribute it to the church members, post it on bulletin boards, or carry it in the church newsletter.

• Plan a worship service around the theme of volunteer ministry.

• Plan a volunteer recognition dinner, invite all volunteers, and honor them with speeches, skits, certificates, awards, gifts.

• Reimburse the out-of-pocket costs volunteers incur as part of their volunteer ministries.

• Ask for a report.

• Send a birthday, anniversary, or Christmas card.

• Provide child care service to enable mothers and fathers of young children to volunteer.

• Keep challenging volunteers.

• Provide good orientation, on-the-ministry training, and continuing education opportunities.

• Provide occasions for volunteers to get together for informal sharing of their experiences.

• Give additional responsibility.

• Send newsworthy information about the work of volunteers to local newspapers.

• Have a party for volunteers.

• Create pleasant surroundings for their work and meetings.

• Take time to talk with volunteers and express appreciation for their efforts.

• Share the positive comments you hear about volunteers and their work with them.

• Provide scholarships and expense money for volunteers to attend training and continuing education workshops.

• Write them thank-you notes.

- Celebrate outstanding projects and achievements.
- Provide good resources and equipment for their use.
- Praise volunteers to their friends.
- Provide opportunities for individual conferences.
- Maintain an accurate record of their training and work and be prepared to provide a reference for the volunteers when they seek employment or other volunteer ministries.
- Plan a volunteer-of-the-month program or emphasis. For example: September—educational ministry workers; November—conference and association volunteers; January—official board; February—committee members; March—community volunteers; April—choir and music. Recognize these people in the church newsletter, the Sunday morning worship service, by placing their pictures on the church bulletin board.
- Send a letter of appreciation to the person's family.
- Honor groups and the individuals in the groups.
- Have a picnic for volunteers.
- Say "Thank you!"
- Smile.
- Publicize information concerning recognition that members of the church have received for their volunteer work in other groups, institutions, or agencies.
- Ask volunteers to write statements on "Why I serve in the church" and publish them in the church newsletter.
- Give a gift of appreciation, for example, a certificate of recognition, a book, or other memento appropriate to their ministry.
- Provide opportunities for volunteers to assess their satisfactions, needs, learnings, and growth in ministry.
- Form volunteer support groups for sharing joys and concerns.
- Provide opportunities for members to develop or create ministries to match and use their skills and interests.

Reprinted by permission from "Supporting Volunteers" in the series *The Ministry of Volunteers*. © 1979, Office for Church Life and Leadership, United Church of Christ.

Adult Learners

When working with adult learners, remember that:
- adults need to participate actively in the learning process.
- adults have a good deal of experience and that experience is a major resource for learning.
- adults need to be free to explore resources in the light of their own interests.

63

- adults learn when they are solving problems or making decisions.
- adults learn when their own need, curiosity, or hunger impels them in a particular direction.
- adults resist and avoid situations where they are treated like children.
- adults want learning to be practical, relevant, related to life as they know it.
- adults do not learn well when they feel threatened or self-conscious.
- adults want to be respected and affirmed.
- adults are not children.
- adults commit to learning when they share responsibility for planning and carrying out an experience.
- adults participate for many reasons—growth, relationships, skills, etc.
- adults want to learn, to become more competent.
- adults can have fun learning.

From "Congregational Workbook," *Volunteerism in the Church* workshops, Division for Life and Mission in the Congregation of the American Lutheran Church, 1980. Developed by Marianne Wilkenson, Hollis Renewal Center, Kansas City, Mo.

Controlling/evaluating

Evaluation is the tool most often neglected by church groups. This is because there are so many myths (mistaken notions) about what evaluation is and does. Let's examine and put to rest some of those myths:

Myth 1:   *Evaluations are apt to be destructive because they point out our faults and failures.*

Fact: Evaluations, to be valid, highlight both "well dones" and "opportunities for improvement."

Myth 2:   *Evaluations are purely statistical and boring.*

Fact: Feelings and comments about what has happened often are more valuable than figures.

Myth 3:   *Evaluation is something done by specialists.*

Fact: Everyone who has been involved in a project or program should be involved in evaluating it.

Myth 4:   *Evaluation is an end in itself, a final report to wrap up a project.*

Fact: Evaluations are only valuable if they are fed into next year's planning process to help you decide what to add, drop, change, or keep.

It is important to do both *objective* program evaluation and *subjective* evaluations to determine how people felt about their participation.

An objective evaluation is very simple if you have planned well. Simply review all of your objectives for the year and determine if your congregation or parish, and the committees and boards within it, accomplished what they set out to do—on time and within budget. If they did not, try to determine why and feed what you learn into next year's planning process. The evaluation may reveal that you wrote a worthwhile objective but did not allow enough time or did not have the right person in charge, or that the need for a certain program no longer exists, so you can drop or change that objective next year.

The subjective evaluation is more difficult and rarely is done in congregations or parishes. It is nonetheless essential if we are to be responsible for our people as well as programs. We must know whether our members grew or were diminished as persons in the process of their involvement; whether their ideas were sought or ignored; whether or not they received the support, training, and recognition they needed; and whether or not they felt they were truly in ministry. It is essential that we hold one another accountable; after all, we are about some very important business. Sloppy work, unfulfilled commitments, procrastination, and unhealthy attitudes must be confronted if we truly are going to care enough to help one another grow. Appendix G, "Report and Evaluation of a Volunteer Ministry" (page 134) can help you in your evaluation process.

Dietrich Bonhoeffer, in his book *Life Together,* suggests the critical questions we need to ask of any Christian community to ascertain whether or not it is on target:

Has the fellowship served to make the individual free, strong, and mature, or has it made him [or her] weak and dependent? Has it taken him by the hand for awhile in order that he may learn to walk by himself or has it made him uneasy and unsure? This is one of the most searching and critical questions that can be put to any Christian fellowship.[10]

Resources recommended for help in understanding tools for management and training are:

The Effective Management of Volunteer Programs, Marlene Wilson, 1976, Volunteer Management Assoc., 279 So. Cedar Brook, Boulder, Colo. 80302.

The Ministry of Volunteers: A Guidebook for Churches, Office for Church Life and Leadership, United Church of Christ, Church Leadership Resources, P.O. Box 179, St. Louis, Mo. 63166.

Recruiting and Developing Volunteer Leaders, George Scheitlin and Eleanore Gillstrom, Parish Life Press, Philadelphia, Pa.

Notes

1. Marlene Wilson, *The Effective Management of Volunteer Programs,* Volunteer Management Associates, 1976, p. 39.
2. Richard Morris, "It's Time to Do Less for Your Church Members," *Ministry, A Magazine for Clergy,* Jan. 1982, p. 4.
3. Elizabeth O'Connor, *Search for Silence,* Word, 1972, p. 106.
4. Wilson, p. 102.
5. Elizabeth O'Connor, *Letters to Scattered Pilgrims,* Harper and Row, 1979, p. 108.
6. Milton Mayerhoff, *On Caring,* Harper and Row, 1971, p. 56.
7. Carl Rogers, quoted in *Bridges Not Walls,* John Stewart, ed., Addison-Wesley, 1973, p. 255.
8. Rueben Gornitzka, *Who Cares?* p. 38.
9. Dietrich Bonhoeffer, *Life Together,* Harper and Row, 1954, p. 49.
10. Bonhoeffer, p. 88.

Chapter 4

Where Do We Begin?
The Plan

I am not much of a believer in pat answers or magic formulas. Therefore, as a writer and trainer, I try to avoid giving out either one. Have you ever gone to a fair or carnival where there was a booth you could enter and become an "instant artist"? In the booth is a cylinder to which you attach a piece of paper, several pots of paint from which you can choose, and a switch that starts the cylinder spinning. You sprinkle your choices of paint on the twirling paper and emerge with your own original artistic masterpiece.

Learning should be like that—the trainer or author should point out the pots of paint available to help you (e.g., principles of management, motivation, etc.), but you need to determine which fit your situation. In other words, you need to choose which colors to use and how long to let it spin. You are the expert in your situation. Since no two situations are alike, each participant or reader should emerge from the experience with his or her own unique picture.

Since I firmly believe that, I am tempted to leave any further planning for implementation of a volunteer ministries program up to you and your particular parish or congregation. However, in training events I have conducted with teams from congregations of varying sizes and from many geographical areas and denominations, I have been urged to go one step further. Participants consistently have requested a tentative outline or action plan that they then could adapt to their own situation. They seemed to feel a need for at least a rough road map to help them begin. This chapter will provide that. Still, it will be essential for you to make choices and adaptations so your plan fits your situation.

Step 1

Appoint a volunteer ministries task force or steering committee. This group would oversee the organization, implementation, promotion, and evaluation of a volunteer ministries program designed to meet the specific needs of your congregation or parish.

The size of this task force should vary depending on the size of your congregation, but is is important to keep it functional (6 to 12 persons). *Members should be chosen carefully.* Not only should they be knowledgeable about the church and its members, but also committed to a fuller utilization of the gifts of all members. Their enthusiasm for the program will be crucial. Suggested types of members are: pastor, president of the church council, liaisons with stewardship committee, religious education department, women's and youth groups, and someone who is a director of a volunteer program in a human service agency in the community (hospital, Red Cross, welfare, school, etc.). The members must be willing to consider this program a major priority for at least one year (preferably two) and attend meetings at least once a month (possibly more frequently at first).

This task force should be responsible to the governing body of the church (which may choose to sanction it under the auspices of an already-existing committee or board). It is important to determine where the task force fits in your structure so it can have legitimacy and access to the church governing body and key leaders.

An orientation meeting should be held to acquaint the members with the concepts covered in Chapters 1, 2, and 3 of this book. Time should be spent exploring the theology of involvement, the present situation in your congregation, and the challenges ahead. A worksheet that might prove helpful is "Volunteers in My Congregation" (Chapter 2, page 39).

Step 2

Set goals, objectives, and action plans for the year. The next step is for your task force to arrive at a goal or mission statement. This is your "reason for being" and must be determined before any further planning can be done. Such a statement needs to be broad and visionary. Here are two examples:

> The purpose of the volunteer ministries program is to both extend and deepen the life of this congregation and to more fully actualize our theology of the priesthood of all believers. Our goal is to enable each person in the congregation (1) to discover and use his or her unique gifts as a child of God; and (2) to grow as a caring person, sharing his or her time and skills with other members, with this church, and with the community.

> The purpose of the volunteer ministries program is to enrich this church's mission through voluntary service by providing more members opportunities to serve as volunteers in the congregation and the community and by improving and coordinating our systems of recruiting, training, supporting, and affirming our members and volunteers.

It is terribly important for your task force to work on this goal statement until it is something you can all say yes to before proceeding further.

As we learned in the last chapter, you then need to break this large goal or mission down into measurable, achievable, short-range objectives. There are any number of different possibilities at this point, based on the needs and realities of your group. I suggest your task force (and other key congregational leaders, if possible) complete Appendix II (page 136), an excellent questionnaire that will provide you with a clear assessment of the needs and strengths of your congregation at present.

In analyzing and discussing the results of this needs assessment, your task force needs to determine several things. Ask yourself these questions: What is our congregation already doing well? What areas need a great deal of work? (List them in order of priority.) How can our task force best organize to help meet these priority needs?

A task force may consider several options when organizing to meet the needs of a congregation. Task force members could divide up the major tasks among themselves and get other congregational members to assist them. Each task force member would take responsibility for a different aspect of the work (e.g., writing volunteer ministries job descriptions, identifying volunteers, training volunteers). This makes the task force a working group instead of a policy group and may be a good option for smaller and newer congregations.

The task force may decide it wants to determine program and policy decisions and priorities and utilize present committees and structures to implement the program (an existing nominating committee will prepare volunteer job descriptions and identify and match volunteers to appropriate jobs, the church council will write the mission statement of the church if one does not already exist, the education committee will develop and conduct training events for volunteers). Instead of doing the work, the task force will see that it is done and done effectively. (This sometimes is a difficult option, for you are changing tradition and other leaders' job descriptions).

The task force may determine the area of greatest need and make that the primary focus for six months or a year. For example, if no job descriptions presently exist, the task force may want to spend several months preparing well-defined job descriptions. Or it may want to begin by establishing a program to improve the present time and talent surveys, including designing and implementing a system of follow-up and placement. The task force may decide the greatest priority lies in enabling members to do volunteer ministries in the community. In that case a survey of community volunteer needs and linking procedures would be in order.

Your task force may determine it needs to find a coordinator or director for the volunteer ministries program to staff the project and devote his or her time and energy to organizing and administering the details of the program. *(This currently is the option that many churches are choosing and the one I most strongly recommend).* This person can be either paid or volunteer and usually works at least half time. The coordinator is accountable to the task force but reports as staff to the senior pastor. The task force then devotes its energies to guiding, advising, supporting, and promoting the program in all aspects of congregational life.

As you can see, the objectives and action plans would vary considerably depending on which option is chosen.

Once the task force determines its priorities and the way it wants to function, the next crucial step is to write a number of *s*pecific, *m*easurable, *a*chievable, and *c*ompatible (SMAC) objectives for the year. To complete the planning phase, an action plan must be developed for each objective to determine *who* will be responsible, *how* they will proceed, *when* each step will be completed (time line), and *what* the cost will be. (See Chapter 3, page 51, for more details.)

Step 3

Inform the governing body and congregation of your plans. It is now important that the task force inform the church council or governing body of its goals, objectives, and plans so it can obtain approval and commitment. This governing body will need to understand and concur with the option chosen for implementation (especially if you plan to change present structures or add a coordinator to the staff). You may find a phasing process to be useful, starting with the first three options and projecting the fourth option (coordinator of volunteer ministries) in one or two years. You would then present both short- and long-range plans, first asking for specific approval for the short-range plans. Our congregation started with: (1) a pilot project of interviewing 25 percent of our members one-to-one to determine each person's gifts and needs, and (2) getting 50 percent of our job descriptions written. By the second year we were ready to propose a half-time paid coordinator to utilize and coordinate all of the information that had been generated. The need was apparent by then.

It is important to help your congregation and its leaders understand the uniqueness of this program. It is *not* another program to compete with religious education, youth groups, women's groups, stewardship, evangelism, etc. *It is the one program intended to enable all the others.* None of the others can function without people, and it is the purpose of the volunteer ministries program to find, enable, and support members who have suitable gifts and interests to serve in all those other programs, as well as in volunteer ministries in the community. The congregation must be helped to see it as a collaborative rather than a competitive venture, or your proposals will meet with resistance.

Step 4

Select a coordinator of the volunteer ministries program.   If your church's governing body has chosen and approved the fourth option, adding a coordinator, it is now time to find that person. Many congregations and parishes have added this staff position when they realized the extent and importance of the problems raised in Chapter 2. Although in the past people have been aware of problems such as pillars and pew-sitters, no job descriptions, and little or no training for volunteers, there has been no one with the time or the specific training to remedy the situation. Pastors and lay leaders alike are already functioning at the edge of burnout, so the dilemma has persisted. Therefore, many congregations/parishes are finding the combination of a task force and a volunteer coordinator the most hopeful and productive option.

Just as the choice of task force members is crucial, so is the selection of a coordinator. This person not only must have the time to devote to the program, but also the commitment, faith, energy, and ability to sell it to others. He or she must see this as a unique and pivotal opportunity for ministry that can profoundly affect the whole church. It is *not* a glorified clerk/typist position.

In Appendix I (page 142) you will find sample job descriptions for this position. Some of the other titles used are: congregational commitment coordinator, congregational care coordinator, and director of the volunteer ministries program.

The position should be widely advertised among the members. The pastor and two or three task force members can be the selection committee. Most congregations require that the applicants be members, but a few have hired people with volunteer management skills who were not members, and this also works out well.

Three critical cautions to be aware of after the coordinator is chosen are:

1. It is important that the task force continue and not abdicate its involvement in the program. First, it is too big a job for one person,

and second, he or she will need the support, advice, and influence of the task force members and other church leaders to get the job done.

2. Be sure the person chosen is considered a full and legitimate member of the church staff (whether the position is paid or volunteer). It will be essential to have weekly or biweekly meetings with the pastor(s) and other staff so that the volunteers' ministries can be integrated into the ongoing life of the church. Internal decisions should be made as needs arise as to who should minister in particular situations—a pastor, a lay leader, or a member who has been identified as having the gift needed. Members' needs and gifts will constantly surface as this program proceeds (that is its very purpose), and these must be shared and acted on weekly.

3. It is very important that this person consciously model the enabler leadership style versus the doer model. He or she must be encouraged to utilize other member volunteers in all aspects of implementation of the program, from setting up retrieval and records systems and typing to interviewing members, training volunteers, etc. The coordinator must demonstrate to other leaders how to tap into the incredible variety of skills and interests of today's church members to help enrich a program. Effective delegation will not only enable this ambitious program to be accomplished, but it will help keep the coordinator and task force from burning out.

Step 5

Plan a retreat for all key leaders in your church.   It is extremely important that the decision makers, committee and program chairpersons, deacons, and church staff not only understand and support the program goals of this project, but also truly catch the vision, philosophy, and theology. The reason this is crucial is that in order to involve more members in the ministry of the congregation, the leaders (pillars) will have to relinquish some power and change their style of leadership from boss, expert, and doer to enabler.

This is a revolutionary break from tradition and practice. It therefore needs to be dealt with honestly and openly. It is disastrous to have more gifts identified and offered and still have people not being called on or utilized. (In one church, after the first year of

73

the program, the number of members who signed up for the evangelism committee soared from 3 to over 30, but the chairman did not change his style of leadership and thus none of the 30 was used. He remained a doer, and it therefore made the program a travesty.)

It is normal to resist change, so this retreat is intended to help alleviate fears, identify useful behavior changes, and provide support for those involved. A format and agenda for such a retreat might be as follows:

Leadership Retreat

Participants   Volunteer ministries task force as conveners; pastors; key decision makers (e.g., church council members, elders, deacons); church staff; chairpersons of program areas and committees.

Preparation   It would be helpful if participants were asked to read one or more of the following resources before the retreat:
1. Chapters 1 and 2 of this book.
2. *Gifts of Grace,* Mary R. Schramm, Augsburg, 1982.
3. *Christianity and Real Life,* William Diehl, Fortress Press, 1976.

Agenda

1. *The theology of involvement.*   For opening devotions, use some of the scripture quotations from Chapter 1 (pages 14-15) relating to the body of Christ and the priesthood of all believers, and the Elizabeth O'Connor quotation relating to gifts (page 23).

2. *The reality in our congregation/parish.*   Have participants fill out and discuss "Volunteers in My Congregation" (Chapter 2, page 39). Task force members may share information regarding common problems covered in Chapter 2 of this book (pages 21-43). They also may share observations relating to the reality in Chapter 1, i.e., Svendsbye, Feucht, McClellan, etc. (pages 16-17).

3. *The challenge.*   Have participants complete the following "Gripe to Goal" exercise:

Step 1   My major gripe, frustration or anxiety about our con-generation's/parish's present use of volunteers is . . .

Step 2   Think about the above sentence and write:
My *real* concern (underlying my frustration) is . . .

Step 3   Now turn the concern into a wish by completing the following sentence:
What I really am wishing for is . . .

Step 4   Then complete the following sentence:
Therefore, my goal for this church's volunteer ministry program is . . .

After they have completed the exercise, have them share concerns and goals (either in small groups that then report to the full group or in the full group). Record and combine their concerns into priority concerns and goals for the group.

Follow the exercise and discussion with a presentation by the volunteer ministries task force on their goals and objectives for the year and how their goals address the concerns and goals identified by the entire group (tie in as directly as possible). Allow time for discussion.

4. *The changes.* This segment is meant to address the changes in attitudes, leadership styles, and roles that will be required on the part of both clergy and lay leaders to make the plan work.

Begin with a short discussion of climate and norms (see pages 37-41). Jenks and Steele remind us that "each person is an enforcer of norms [the unwritten rules of how we relate to one another] . . . we contribute to the strength of a norm by what we are willing to let others enforce unchallenged, since our silence signals tacit approval. By both our actions and nonactions we are all enforcers and creators of the norms (and climate) that each of us feels in a group or organization."[1] *So, if we want changes, we are all responsible to make them happen.*

This is essential for church leaders to understand if, as leaders, we are to change disabling behaviors into enabling ones. Some quotes may help:

75

. . . the degree to which I can create relationships which facilitate the growth of others as separate persons is a measure of the growth I have achieved in myself.

Carl Rogers
On Becoming a Person

To care for another person in the most significant sense is to help him grow and actualize himself.

Milton Mayeroff
On Caring

Sin is our failure to grant another his plea for community.

Martin Buber

An intimate relation between people not only asks for mutual openness but also for mutual respectful protection of each other's uniqueness.

Henri Nouwen
Reaching Out

Identify the need for creative problem solving to change gripes into goals. Have participants complete the worksheet, "Are You—or Can You Be—a Creative Leader/Manager?" (see Appendix J, page 145). Then have them share in pairs the traits each of them sees in the other that each wishes to develop in himself or herself. Have them help each other learn how those traits were developed. If there is time, discuss "Blocks to Creativity" (see Appendix K, page 147) in the full group.

Discuss the information from Chapter 2 on leadership styles (pages 24-28) and motivation (pages 28-37). Emphasize the need to match the *right* person to the *right* job (McClelland and Herzberg). This is extremely important information for the participants to understand.

Practice delegation (the key to the enabler style of leadership) by completing the following activities.

• Have the participants write a job description for some part of their present leadership job they might be willing to delegate to someone else. Urge them to make it something significant.

(Use Appendix L, page 149—a job description form—and review the chart in Appendix A.)

Debrief the experience in small groups, using "Resistance to Change" (Appendix M, page 150). Which of these resistances did they experience or do they anticipate as they try to delegate more responsibility to others? How can these resistances be minimized?

Discuss the role of the pastor(s) as it would be affected by this program. Which resistances does he or she feel or anticipate?

• *Care Power* exercise. Have participants list the three people in their entire lives who have had the most positive influences on them. Ask, "Is one a relative, one a mentor or teacher, one a friend?" (The usual response is a combination of those three.) "What did they all have in common? Why were they so influential?" (Responses usually are: "They cared, were supportive, helped me be my best, held me accountable, saw potential in me, were honest with me.") Point out that *care power* is the longest-lasting power in the world. This is especially important to remember as parents and leaders.

Complete the activities by going over "Characteristics of a Servant/Leader" (Appendix N, page 150).

5. *The plan of action.* Have the group define the ministry of leadership in their church. Discuss how they will measure their success as lay leaders and clergy. Will they measure success by how many hours they personally devote to their area of responsibility or will they judge by how many others they are able to involve and grow in their area of responsibility?

Have each participant complete the "Personal Plan of Action Worksheet" (Appendix O, page 151). An optional activity would be to share their worksheets with one other person and sign each other's self-contracts.

Close the session by reading the quotes relating to leadership (Chapter 2, pages 27-28) and leading the group in prayer.

Step 6

Anticipate and understand attitudinal blocks. Since I began this chapter by stating this was to be a rough road map, it is appropriate that I also point out some possible problem areas, detours, and "potholes" along the way. These primarily are attitudinal blocks that may surface once a program is implemented. If you do not anticipate attitudinal blocks and work through them, they can keep you from getting where you want and need to go. The following problems are not imaginary or farfetched—they are all based on actual situations. I will present them in the form of scenarios (and you may want to use them as role plays).

Block 1: The volunteer coordinator is not considered a legitimate member of the team

Actors: Volunteer coordinator, senior pastor, assistant pastor, and secretary

Volunteer coordinator   I would find it very helpful if we could set a weekly time when we could all get together and exchange the information and concerns we each have heard concerning our members and then work out ways that one of us or another member of the congregation might minister to these concerns specifically.

Assistant pastor   That's really pretty hard to do, since we all are operating on different schedules.

Senior pastor   There really isn't a time during the week when we all are here at the same time. Our schedules ar constantly shifting.

Secretary   I feel a need to exchange information all together, too. I get telephone calls and sometimes I don't know the information or I'm not sure exactly what the plans are until the last minute. Maybe if we all got together, it would help me to get more lead time on information and be able to "plug in" better.

Assistant pastor   But you do a great job keeping ahead of things, and we both stop in and give you information at least once a day.

Senior pastor   The church doesn't work like other organizations. Its staff just can't set up meetings and stick with them. We've tried before, but it always gets too impossible to maintain.

Volunteer coordinator   I would still like us to set a time for a

78

weekly staff meeting, if only to help me. I feel responsible for the information being shared with me regarding needs and how people want to help. I'm not really sure how to handle it. By meeting, maybe we could discuss how best to minister to the concerns of the week and decide who would be best at dealing with them. I would just feel more relieved if I knew someone was looking into the concerns, and whether or not we were following up more effectively when someone wants to become involved in one of our ministries. I think we let them fall through the cracks too often.

Secretary   I know I would feel better if I knew that some people were being contacted. I feel really bad whenever I type up the church directory and see names of people that I haven't seen at church or church activities for a long time. Maybe they are being contacted, but if they are, I don't get any feedback on it.

Senior pastor   Well, I suppose we could try meeting and see how it works. When do you suppose we could all meet?

(They set a date, but the senior pastor rescheduled the first meeting date as he had scheduled a conflicting meeting.)

Block 2: Threat to the pastor

Actors: Pastor, lay leader

Scene: Pastor's office

Lay leader   I've been meaning to ask you, Pastor, how's our new volunteer coordinator doing? He's been on board here about six months now and I'm curious as to how it's working out.

Pastor   *(hesitantly)* Well . . . by and large, it's going very well. I mean he's very enthusiastic and a real achiever. He's just getting things organized around here right and left! *(Pause)* But sometimes I'm afraid he goes a little bit overboard.

Lay leader   What do you mean?

Pastor   Well, sometimes he kind of strays into my domain. I mean our roles are still pretty fuzzy as far as how we fit together and who's supposed to do what.

Lay leader   That could get frustrating for both of you I'm sure. Give me a "for instance" and maybe I can help.

79

Pastor   Well . . . several times he's actually gotten into *doing ministry* . . . and that's what I'm here for!

Lay leader   What kind of ministry are you talking about? It would help if you'd give me an example.

Pastor   Just last week it happened when Mrs. Peterson died so suddenly. Next thing I knew they'd called him to go talk to the Peterson's teenage daughter—and that was while I was still helping get things straightened out at the hospital. Why didn't they let me know the girl needed help—instead of calling him? After all, I'm the pastor here!

Lay leader   It sounds like you are quite angry about that.

Pastor   Sure I'm angry. I was called to be the pastor. What do you expect me to do—just sit here and let him take charge? The job description says he's responsible to me.

Lay leader   You mean he's not communicating with you?

Pastor   Oh, he does that fine. It's just that he's supposed to locate people, find out what they need, match them up, but I'm supposed to do ministry. That's my job.

Lay leader   So, it's when he starts caring for people that you care for that you get upset.

Pastor   Well, it's just that the congregation gets confused. Pretty soon they won't know where to turn. They will wonder whether to turn to him or me.

Block 3: *Pillars versus pew-sitters*

Actors: Volunteer coordinator, secretary

Volunteer coordinator   Mary, do you have a minute? I've just got to talk to someone!

Secretary   Sure, come on in and have a cup of coffee. The pastors are gone and it's quiet for the moment. What's on your mind?

Volunteer coordinator   It's last night's council meeting. I'm so frustrated, I'm ready to quit!

Secretary   What happened?

Volunteer coordinator   It's not what happened—it's what *didn't* happen . . . again! I'd asked for time on the agenda to report on the results of the one-to-one interviews we've been conducting with the parishioners the last two months. We've discovered

80

so many people who are willing and want to be involved in various committees and programs, and I wanted to remind the various chairpersons about the importance of calling the people I'd referred to them.

Secretary   Sounds great. What happened at the meeting that upset you?

Volunteer coordinator   First of all, I ended up *last* on the agenda again—even after the purchase of a new garden hose! It was after 10:30 and I could tell that all anyone wanted to do was get out of there and go home. But I plunged ahead anyhow. I asked four different committee chairpersons about their results in calling the parishioners I'd referred to their committees and not one of them had followed up on any of them. They all had the usual excuses: "I was too busy!" "I hate getting noes." "It's easier to do it myself." "I hate to ask people—it makes me feel like I'm begging." "No one knows this job like I do" . . . and on and on! Here are these "pew-sitters" everyone gripes about finally volunteering for committees and then no one calls them. It's ridiculous!

Secretary   Boy, I can see why you're upset.

Block 4: Resistance to change

Actors: Volunteer coordinator who has been in job for three years; pastor; three members of volunteerism task force just returned from a "Volunteerism in the Church" workshop which they attended with the pastor and volunteer coordinator.

Pastor   This is our first meeting since the workshop on volunteer ministries. I hope everyone is still as enthused as I am about the immense possibilities of the plan we developed together at the workshop.

Task force member 1   I sure am!

Task force member 2   Can't wait to try out some of those new ideas!

Task force member 3   It was terrific to rethink where we're going with lay ministry and what's really possible.

Volunteer coordinator   You know, when I got back, I had time to realize we're already doing most of it—they just had fancier terms for stuff I've been doing for a long time.

Pastor   Yes, you do have some fine things already underway. But it's always good to take an objective look once in a while and see if we can't improve on a good thing.

Task force member 1   For instance, we've never done personal interviews with our people—we've relied only on time and talent sheets and casual conversations. My hunch is we really don't know a lot of our people.

Volunteer coordinator   When you've worked with them as long as I have, you know them. I just haven't written it all down. But just ask me who's good at almost anything that needs doing and I can tell you in a minute. No sense making things more complicated than they need to be.

In conclusion, let me raise the concern each of you undoubtedly feels. How do you address all of these various challenges? It seems almost overwhelming! I'd like to share a story from Robert Greenleaf's childhood—recounted in his book *Servant Leadership*.[2] It's a story about a dogsled race in his hometown. Most of the boys in the race had big sleds and several dogs. Greenleaf (only five years old) had a small sled and one little dog. The course was one mile staked out on the lake.

As the race started, the more powerful contenders quickly left Greenleaf behind. In fact, he hardly looked like he was in the race at all.

> All went well with the rest until, about halfway around, the team that was second started to pass the team then in the lead. They came too close and the dogs got in a fight.

Pretty soon the other dog teams joined in, and little Greenleaf could see one big seething mass of kids, sleds, and dogs about one half mile away. So he gave them all wide berth, and was the only one that finished the race. He concludes:

> As I reflect on the many vexing problems and the stresses of our times that complicate their solutions, this simple scene from long ago comes vividly to mind. And I draw the obvious moral: *No*

82

matter how difficult the challenge or how impossible or hopeless the task may seem, if you are reasonably sure of your course—just keep going!

Notes

1. Fritz Steele and Stephen Jenks, *The Feel of the Work Place*, Addison-Wesley, 1977, pp. 48-49.
2. Robert K. Greenleaf, *Servant Leadership*, Paulist Press, 1977, pp. 174-175.

Chapter 5

What about the "Yeah, Buts" and "Ain't It Awfuls"?

The Questions

I suspect that at this point many practical, nitty-gritty questions are flooding your mind. For every argument I have made in favor of establishing a volunteer ministries program, you could probably counter with a whole raft of "yeah, buts":

- Our congregation is too small to try this; or
- Our congregation is too big; or
- Our congregation is too old; or
- It makes good sense—but "ain't it awful" our congregation doesn't have anyone with the time to implement it?

Any excuse to opt out of change will do. That's only human nature. Change is difficult and risky—so my hunch is that you are searching for justification to keep things as they are.

Henri Nouwen declares that questions are not only to be tolerated, but embraced.

> Often someone's careful and honest articulation of ambiguities, uncertainties, and painful conditions of life gives us new hope. The paradox is indeed that new life is born out of the pain of the old.[1]

It is not questions that get us into trouble, but rather our failure to listen to them. So this chapter intends to share with you the most commonly articulated questions people have raised at our volunteer ministries workshops. And I will attempt to suggest some possible answers. My hope is that you will find solace in the fact that others have shared some of your concerns.

Questions relating to pillars and pew-sitters

1. *How can we get other members to become more actively involved so we don't keep asking the same faithful few for everything?*

Chapter 2 covers many ideas on how to deal with this problem. Review those relating to job descriptions, recruitment, and interviewing. Following up on time and talent surveys is a *must*. (In a recent Gallup Poll regarding volunteerism, the vast majority of the people who did not volunteer at all last year revealed they had never been asked. So ask!)

2. *Is there a way to ask people to be involved that helps them to say yes rather than no?*

Remember to make the request as personal as possible, linking the person's gifts with an appropriate opportunity. Avoid the "Buffalo Bill," desperate, or guilt methods of recruitment. The "Motivation" section in Chapter 2 pointed out how achievers, affiliators, and power-motivated people respond to different challenges, so by asking the right person for the right job, you will likely receive a yes. Ask new members within the first three months if at all possible. Also, review the checklist (Appendix B, page 126) before making your calls or visits. Be prepared to succeed.

3. *Why are so many people unwilling to do their share? Don't they care about the church?*

They may well have tried to become involved at various times and were overlooked or rejected. (Remember the story of Jane Whosit and Mrs. Oldstandby at the end of Chapter 2?) Also, it is often assumed that when people have said no to one job, they do not want to be involved at all, so they never are asked again. This is where a system of follow-up and referral will help—so people are not lost in the cracks.

4. *Is it because so many women now work outside the home that we're having trouble finding volunteers for church and elsewhere?*

It is true that five to ten years ago the vast majority of volunteers were women and many of them did not work outside the home. However, in the latest Gallup Poll, 41-45 percent of all volunteers in the U.S. and Canada were male. (And 33 percent of all Americans volunteered on a regular basis in 1981.)

One of the reasons fewer women are free to volunteer (at least as frequently or as long as in the past) is that over 50 percent of our women now hold paying jobs.

This does not mean women are not volunteering, but they are more discriminating in where and how they do it. They look for training, support, shared jobs, opportunity for personal growth, and causes that truly make a difference. Both working men and women prefer shorter assignments whenever possible.

Many groups are still only looking for women to volunteer and thus have not joined the many agencies that have tapped into the vast new reservoir of retired persons, youth, men, and people with disabilities. What a rich and diverse potential volunteer work force we have today!

5. *Why do people volunteer?*

There are numerous reasons, which vary for different people. The most common reasons shared by volunteers in interviews and surveys are:

- They want to be needed.
- They want to help others and make a difference.
- They want to learn new skills or use skills they already have.
- They want to belong to a caring community and feel accepted as members.
- They want self-esteem and affirmation.
- They want to grow in their faith and share their God-given gifts.
- They want to keep from being lonely.
- They want to support causes they believe in.

On the other hand, the reasons people say yes when they are *drafted* may be quite different: i.e., feeling guilty, not knowing how to say no, not wanting to let someone down, etc.

Daniel Yankelovitch, the well-known social researcher, stated in his article "New Rules in American Life: Searching for Self-Fulfillment in a World Turned Upside Down" that American adults of the 80s are longing for three things: *commitment, connectedness,* and *creative expression*.[2] This is exciting news, for volunteering, when done effectively, provides all three!

Mary Schramm, in her excellent book *Gifts of Grace,* points out:

> If using our gifts and sensing fulfillment and peace is associated with our work week, we can thank God. Many people find the best use of their gifts does not coincide with how they earn their pay-check. The sense of unfulfillment, caused by that creative being inside us, needs attention, and perhaps it is after the nine-to-five routine that the unrest is quieted. It may be in our leisure hours that we engage in the kind of ministry where we feel free to express our gifts.[3]

I believe this helps explain why the fastest growing source of volunteers nationally is working people. My prayer is that the church may acknowledge this quest for meaning and facilitate the use of gifts on the part of our members.

6. *How can we get the church to become more imaginative in the options for ministry we offer our members?*

I have two suggestions: (a) *Stop* saying "we always do it that way here" and "we never do it that way here." Creativity will begin to flourish: (b) *Start* with your members' gifts and needs and new forms and possibilities of ministry will emerge. People are more important than slots! Our members today not only have incredibly diverse and interesting professional skills to share (computer science, graphics, interior design, human resource management, etc.) but fascinating and unique hobbies as well. The key is not to just maintain our life together, but to enrich it.

7. *Can time and talent surveys be effective?*

They can be, but usually are not. First of all, most of them need to be redesigned to appear more appealing, be more informative, and offer more options. They also need to have a section for volunteer ministries in the community.

Yet, no matter how good the form is, they are still a disaster if no one follows up on the information received. If they are ignored they become the exact antithesis of all we've been talking about. People's gifts are rejected through neglect, and that must not happen. Therefore, the key to making them effective is threefold:

a. Have a system of retrieval so the information gets to the proper chairperson or staff person;

b. Have a system of follow-up to be sure that the names referred actually were contacted. If one area of ministry is full, the person should still be called and referred elsewhere.

c. Remember one-to-one interviews always are more effective in helping people tell you who they are and the gifts they have to share.

8. *What if the wrong person volunteers for a job?*

First of all, the person isn't wrong, the job is wrong for that person. I repeatedly have emphasized the importance of matching the right person to the right job. Recruitment should not be viewed as taking the first hand that's raised or the first warm body through the door. Recruitment is simply an invitation to come in and chat with an appropriate person (i.e., volunteer coordinator, pastor, or committee chairperson) about your needs and the individual's gifts and finding that right match. There is a place for everyone—that's what "whole body theology" is all about.

If there is a mismatch, then whoever is in charge needs either to train the person, transfer them to a more appropriate job, or change the job.

9. *Is our nominating system in some church bodies backwards (i.e., the nominating committee recruits people willing to serve on the church council and it is not until* after *they are elected that they decide who will chair which committees or boards)?*

In my opinion, yes. This process violates everything we have discussed regarding calling people to serve in areas in which they are gifted. This is especially troublesome when we realize we are choosing our leaders this way. Every leadership job should have a clearly written job description, including the gifts and characteristics of the person needed to fill it. These descriptions ought to be the basis for the nominating process. The committee should *seek out* those in the congregation/parish with the gifts needed, and nominate them for the appropriate office. This would greatly improve the quality of leadership in the church.

The all too familiar scene of newly elected leaders selecting chairpersons for the year based on turns, oughts, or who is not there to say no must be changed.

Questions relating to gifts

1. *How do we help people discover their gifts, especially those who don't feel they have any?*

We need to bring new life and meaning to what we declare about our theology of the priesthood of all believers and of gifts (see Chapter 1). We can only do this by living out what we declare by:

a. treating our members as unique and valuable children of God, individual in their gifts and possibilities;
b. becoming enablers or servant leaders who demonstrate that people are as important as programs;
c. asking our members about their gifts, listening, and then acting on what they tell us;
d. watching when they "light up" and get excited ("Enjoyment of a task, though not the only criterion, is a clue to identifying the gifts that were given us." [4]);
e. affirming the achievers, affiliators, and power people in our midst. They all need affirmation, and we need all of them; and
f. *celebrating gifts*, yours and other people's!

2. *Do people like to volunteer the skills they use in their paid work (i.e., accounting, carpentry, teaching, writing, computer programming, etc.)?*

There used to be a myth around that you were never to ask volunteers to do what they did for pay—that they all wanted a change of pace. My experience is that you cannot assume that to be true today. Some people love to do what they do professionally and want to share that "best gift" with their church; others are not allowed to do their best, most creative work at their paid job due to hierarchical restrictions and want to have a chance to fulfill this need in their volunteer ministry. Still others really do want to do something totally different (like the executive who gets renewed planting shrubs or helping with a pancake breakfast). The best advice, therefore, is do not assume anything. Ask!

3. *How does a lay person with professional skills utilize them as a volunteer at church without threatening the pastor?*

I cannot tell you how frequently variations of this question are raised. It is an immense problem in today's church, and far too many of our lay people who have been unable to find a way to deal with it have taken their time and talents elsewhere, where they feel appreciated and valued.

My concern here is that I do not believe seminaries are equipping pastors to understand their role as facilitators, enablers, supporters, and shepherds of the gifts of the body. Rather, they are trained to be "doers"; thus their feelings of turf and threat enter in where they should not. Ministry is the work of the whole priesthood and it involves proclaiming, teaching, worshiping, loving, witnessing, and serving.[5] Certainly no one person can do that alone—even the pastor.

It is essential that we begin to deal honestly with this in our leadership training for laity and clergy alike. Far too many pastors are burning out and leaving the ministry, while competent lay people at the same time are leaving in disaffection. The key is to concentrate on persons versus roles and gifts versus turf.

4. *How can I get out of a volunteer job I'm tired of doing (especially one I'm good at)?*

This is where having definite time commitments on the job description helps. Once you have fulfilled your agreed upon commitment, the leadership must renegotiate that job with you. If you want a change, this is your chance to say so. The leader in turn should release you, gratefully saying, "Thank you, and God bless you for your service" (not invoking guilt by saying, "But we don't have anyone else—you won't let us down, will you?").

5. *How can I let people know what I'm good at doing without appearing pushy or vain?*

It is almost impossible to let people know about your talents without telling them directly unless there is a system of interviewing of some kind, where questions of talent are asked. Another method to make public individuals' talents is to utilize a survey form such as "Discovering My Gifts" (Chapter 3, page 58).

6. *How do I let someone know that I need more training? I'm in a job over my head.*

Tell the person who asked you to do the job, and the sooner the better! Do not feel that it is a sign of incompetence or failure. You care enough to want to do the job well and the leader owes you that right. Training to help people succeed in what they are asked to do is a critical part of the job of leadership.

I will never forget a friend of mine who had always taught kindergarten in Sunday school. One year she was asked to teach a junior high class, and she thought it would be such fun to have students with whom she could really communicate and dialog. Needless to say, it took only two Sundays for her to realize she desperately needed help. She knew nothing about the age group and the students knew it. She felt totally inadequate and didn't know what to do. My advice to her was to tell her leader immediately.

7. *Why hasn't anyone at church ever asked me what I'm good at, what I like and dislike doing, and how I'm trying to grow in my faith? Don't they care about me?*

Ask them.

8. *How can I find out all the options for service in our congregation before I say yes to a specific request? I really want to use my gifts.*

This is the central idea behind setting up a display rack for volunteer ministry descriptions that I suggested in Chapter 3 (page 55). People then have access to information about opportunities and can indicate to the volunteer coordinator (or other designated person or persons) their interest. New members love it! This also helps individuals take care of the problem of letting people know what they do well and like to do.

9. *Is it OK to want and expect to get something back personally from my volunteer experiences?*

People do not stop being human just because they become volunteers, and human beings have legitimate needs. Yes, it is not only

OK, but it is important that you personally get something of value out of the experience.

Review the "Motivation" section of Chapter 2 relating to McClelland, Herzberg, Maslow, and your faith motive. Then look for that need "with your name on it."

10. *Does the church value my volunteer work in the community— and see that as ministry also?*

This varies from denomination to denomination and congregation to congregation. I know I personally have been made to feel like a deserter at times, especially when my ministry in the community has been my primary focus. Some people still do not view that as "real church work."

However, I know that today's church members are seeking validation for their ministry not only in the community, but also in their vocations and occupations. After all, that is what being the scattered church is all about. (Chapter 6 will deal with this in depth.)

One way a church can acknowledge and support scattered ministries is to include them on time and talent surveys. Another idea is to commission and recognize your community volunteers at a special service (or part of a service) during National Volunteer Week in April of each year.

Questions relating to delegation and accountability

1. *What kind of leadership style works best with volunteers?*

What works best depends on the volunteer, and it is the *enabler* who will have the caring and flexibility to change his or her style to fit the needs of the person. Review the material in the "Leadership" section of Chapter 2.

Two things to keep in mind when working with volunteers are:
a. persuading works better than dictating; and
b. people are most committed to plans *they* help make.

2. *I am a chairperson of a committee. Why should I try to get a bunch of other people together for meetings and such when I can do the work quicker alone (and probably better too)?*

It all depends on your philosophy and theology of leadership. Are you a leader to show how much you personally can get done? Or are you a leader to help others grow and use their gifts?

Also, remember the problem of burn out. "Doers" tend to use themselves up, and when they leave, the programs they worked so hard to develop collapse because no one else knows how to do the job. By sharing your work now, you are building for the future of both your program and the people in it.

3. *Why should I delegate? Whenever I've tried it, I've been disappointed.*

I'd like to share some words of wisdom from Tom Knight. I regret I do not know the origin of the quote:

> Isn't it funny, when the other fellow takes a long time to do something, he's slow. When I take a long time to do something, I'm thorough. When the other fellow doesn't do it, he's lazy. When I don't do it, I'm busy. When the other fellow does it without being told, he's overstepping his bounds. When I go ahead and do it without being told, that's initiative. When the other fellow states his opinions strongly, he's bullheaded. When I state my opinion strongly, I'm firm. When the other fellow overlooks a few rules of etiquette, he's rude. When I skip a few rules, I'm doing my own thing.

4. *I'm a perfectionist and it makes me nervous to delegate to people I can't control. Can I hold volunteers accountable, and, if so, how?*

Two of my major premises both in working with volunteers myself and in teaching others to do so have been:

a. *Never lower standards for volunteers.* It is the ultimate putdown for them to feel that what they do is so unimportant that it doesn't even matter if they do it well—or even at all.

b. *View volunteers as nonpaid staff* and always hold them accountable for their commitment.

One way this can be done is to have the job descriptions, goals, objectives, and action plans written and shared with all concerned. Many problems develop simply because of unclear expectations and assumptions.

As a perfectionist you are your own worst enemy (and you

probably are not much fun to work with either). Try being a perfectionist only in those few major things that truly make a difference. William James once observed that the art of being wise is knowing what to overlook.

You can be sure that if you delegate to someone else, they will not do the job the way you do it. They might even do it better and then you can learn from them. Experts claim that the most *influential* people are those who are most influenceable. Think about it.

5. *If a volunteer goofs up, what should I do? Can you ever "fire" them?*

This question eventually surfaces in every volunteer management training session I've ever held.

If you are serious about holding volunteers accountable, and they fail to do the job, have inappropriate attitudes, boss others around or procrastinate repeatedly, then you must take action. Ask yourself, "What would I do if I was paying this person to do this job?" and then do it!

First, you need to review the job description with the individual to see if he or she is clear about what originally was agreed upon. (It's amazing how often this first step clears up the problem.) Second, clarify the problem and be explicit about your expectations. Then examine the alternatives together (i.e., change behavior or attitudes, meet deadlines, change jobs or get needed training, etc.). Finally, choose the alternative on which you both agree, and set a time line to implement and monitor the progress, giving support and affirmation along the way.

If the person either does not follow through even after two to three chances or is nasty about being held accountable as a volunteer, I would "fire" them. Remember the "Care Power" exercise in Chapter 4. If you keep rescuing them, you will both lose.

6. *As a pastor in two small rural churches, I need and want to delegate more to my parishioners. But they resist, saying that's all the pastor's job. I'm burning out. What can I do?*

Share the whys of involvement from Chapter 1. The parishioners must be helped to see that they too are ministers and they are shirking their jobs (and their opportunities). They remind me of the people that Feucht describes as viewing the church as a spectator sport: a place where they can come to get a holy dose of sedative. This is contrary to theology we declare as Christians, and the people need to come to grips with that. Consider trying a retreat similar to the one outlined in Chapter 4.

Most important of all, you must be able to face up to your own feelings about this and express them. It will make you vulnerable, but isn't that what it means to be a Christian?

Norman Vincent Peale once observed, "In any worthwhile endeavor there is an element of risk. You may run into opposition, you may be laughed at. But you have to be willing to be vulnerable—to be, if necessary, a fool for God, knowing that the rewards of righting a wrong, or improving your world, far outweigh the possible risks or hazards."

And a wise teacher once advised, "Behold the turtle—he makes progress only when he sticks his neck out!"

7. *If I decide to try to delegate more significant responsibility to someone else, how do I know who to give the job to?*

This depends on both the job and your strengths and weaknesses. (We all have both and the wise leader knows this well).

Is this a job that requires organization or problem-solving skills? Look for an achiever. Will it require nurturing and caring skills? Find an affiliator. Do you need influence and impact? You need a power person.

It is good to have a well-rounded team, so you need to find those people who can "round you out." In the movie *Rocky*, Rocky says to his fiancee, "You got gaps and I got gaps. Let's fill each other's gaps!" That's what is called *synergy*—being better together than either one can be alone. How we need synergistic teamwork in the church!

8. *If our parish decides to appoint a volunteer ministries coordinator, how can we help ensure that he or she will become a legitimate member of our ministry team?*

The volunteer ministries task force must play a pivotal role in seeing that the pastor(s) and lay leaders understand the volunteer

96

ministries program and the role of the coordinator *philosophically and psychologically,* as well as *pragmatically.* My opinion is that this can best be done at a retreat like the one suggested in Chapter 4.

9. *How can we shape up those awful church council meetings that go on forever and get nothing done? Also, how do we keep from meeting just out of habit?*

Read the material in Chapter 2 relating to achievers and affiliators and how they conduct meetings. Then modify your own behavior and confront that of others. I, personally, use a simple three-point method to help keep the meeting on target:

a. Early in a meeting, if I am unclear about the purpose, I ask "Why are we here and what is the agenda?"
b. Midway through, if I'm unclear about what we have accomplished, I say, "I wonder if we might summarize where we are and what we have done thus far?"
c. At the end of the meeting, when everyone brings out calendars for that inevitable next meeting, I ask "Why do we need to meet again?" (If no one knows, I don't go).

You have no idea how many people have thanked me privately for playing the role of critical questioner.

Questions relating to burnout

1. *How do I tell my church that I am tired and need to stop my over-involvement for awhile. I am so close to burning out. How do I say no without feeling guilty?*

This is an often expressed plea on the part of both "pillars" and clergy.

This poem by a friend, Lyman Randall, expresses the feelings of futility and frustration so well:

No Time

If only I had more time,
I would stop and listen to you.
If only I had more time,
I might try something new.

If only I had more time,
I could rest my load awhile.

If only I had more time,
I might return your smile.

If the day had more hours,
I might get everything done.
And then I could take some time
To enjoy some hard-earned fun.

I hope I have some time
To spend before I die
To figure where my years went
And why I want to cry.

But no time now for tears
Nor any time for prayers
No time to calm my fears
   No time
     No time
      No time!

I know this problem intimately, as I came perilously close to a classic stress-related collapse several years ago. It was terrifying. I felt like people were "using me up" and I was unable to stop it. The situation seemed to be out of control and I felt sure I was heading for a physical or emotional breakdown. Then my family and a couple of good friends confronted me with the incredible fact that it was my problem and asked me when I was going to take care of it. (I had been hoping *they* would do something about it!) I decided to go on a three-day retreat by myself and try to sort things out.

The following is an excerpt from my personal journal, August 15, 1979.[6]

I am still at the condominium I rented at Keystone Lodge. I awoke about 6:30 to sun streaming through my window. Unhappily I missed the sunrise which I'd enjoyed yesterday. I spent a half hour in devotions and meditation. Somehow God seems within such easy reach here.

Before breakfast, I decided to take a walk around the lake. What a contrast this walk was to the one I'd taken my first day here. Was it really only two days ago? That walk was "driven"! I knew "I needed exercise," that "walking reduces tension," that it was more practical for me than jogging due to my weight and temperament —and finally, maybe after a walk, I'd be able to settle down to some serious thinking. After all . . . that's why I am really here. So I walked . . . briskly, blindly, and with grim determination.

This morning I walked briskly . . . between stops. The stops were to enjoy a beaver, a chipmunk eating a Lifesaver, five kinds of birds, a flock of ducks, several varieties of wild flowers, a dandelion floating on the lake, and a school of trout swimming by the shore. The lake and the path are the same . . . only I have changed. My senses are alive and sharpened to sounds, smells, and sights I've missed these past few months. How sad to go through life too busy to enjoy it—allowing perceptual blinders to filter out the world's beauty!

Now I'm sitting on a bench between the lake and a stream, writing while enjoying the warmth of the sun. I find it almost impossible to put into words the tremendous difference these three days have made in how I *feel*—about myself, others, and my work. Perhaps the best way is to contrast the emotions and feelings I experienced the last several weeks before this retreat and those I am experiencing now. Both may sound extreme—even exaggerated—but they were very real to me:

Before	After
Overwhelmed	Centered
Out of control	Renewed energy
Loss of energy (very rare for me)	Values—goals clarified
No enthusiasm	Rested
Resentful	Relaxed
Distrustful	Productive
Martyred	Eager
Trouble with words (and words are my business)	Calm
Loss of sensory perception	Senses sharp
Fatigue	Humor returned
Trouble sleeping	Ready for whatever comes
Annoyed at small things	Hopeful
Eating-drinking too much	I like me better!
Loss of humor	
Pain in the neck	

The amazing thing to me is that I also got so much productive, creative work accomplished. It was far from only "navel gazing." Some of the tangible outcomes of these three days are:

- A statement of my values and an action plan to implement changes

- Reorganization of my company
- A rewrite of Chapter 1 of my book
- A book on power read
- One-half of a novel read and enjoyed
- A training session planned and outlined

In other words, I accomplished in three short days several projects I'd been floundering with for weeks. How about that for cost-effectiveness!

I now realize I had been on the edge of a precipice—with only a toehold to keep me from crashing into a physical or emotional collapse. That has never happened to me before, and now that I know how frightening and debilitating it can be, I vow never to let it happen again. I also realize it is my problem to see that it doesn't.

When I look at the results of these few short days, I realize this has been one of the smartest investments of my life. There is no such thing as not being able to afford the time or the money to do this when needed. I can never again afford not to.

What I had experienced was a full-fledged assault by the subtle killer known as stress. It is quietly and relentlessly waging its war on people of all ages across this country. It buries its victims daily —but it carefully hides behind the declared villains of heart disease, strokes, cancer, ulcers, etc. Therefore, few know of its deadly nature.

The process I used to accomplish this seeming miracle was quite simple.

a. I listed the 8-10 things I valued most in life;

b. I prioritized them by deciding which would be most difficult to give up if I were to have a health breakdown;

c. I then objectively analyzed my calendar for the past year and found the cause of my stress was primarily that my time and my values were not together. Sixty percent of my time and most of my prime time was spent on the last four items of my values list. This caused a tremendous sense of frustration and guilt regarding what I was unable to give to my most important values (mine were my God, my family, and myself).

d. I wrote specific, measurable objectives for each item on my values list regarding what I intended to add, drop, or change to deal with the problem, and by when.

e. I spent the next six to twelve months doing what I had determined needed to be done. Things no longer were out of control and it felt great.

I now know that being a good steward means taking care of me —physically, emotionally, spiritually, and intellectually. I urge you to do the same for you. (See the article entitled "Stress Management: A Necessary Survival Tool for Today's Professional," Appendix P, page 154.) If you need professional help, be sure and get it. Stress kills people.

2. As a pastor, how can I keep the congregation from owning me to the point that I have little or no time for myself or my family? I'm afraid my marriage is in trouble.

Here again, you must be honest about your own limitations and needs. An amazing number of people still believe the clergy only really works on Sunday (as that's when they see you). You must help them understand all the endless demands on your time and energies (not only during the normal eight-hour workday, but evenings as well). If you finally admit that you cannot be all things to all people, it may just allow some others to share more of the load. They can't help if you won't give it up.

What is biblical about driving families apart? It is contrary to everything we say we believe. Your family is as important as anyone else's. Nurture it lovingly and carefully. It should be a top priority.

The theologian Martin Marty, in a *Reader's Digest* article entitled "Simplify Your Life," stated:

> All truly deep people have at the core of their being the genius to be simple and to know how to seek simplicity, the inner and the outer aspects of their lives match . . . they are so uncluttered by any self-importance within and so unthreatened from without that they have what one philosopher calls a certain "availability" . . . successful living is a journey towards simplicity and a triumph over confusion.[7]

And Pope John XXIII, in his book *Journal of a Soul,* observes:

> The older I grow, the more clearly I perceive the dignity and winning beauty of simplicity in thought, conduct, and speech;

a desire to simplify all that is complicated and to treat everything with the greatest naturalness and clarity.[8]

Summary

Questions, questions, questions. They seem endless. Nouwen reminds us to "be patient toward all that is unsolved in your heart and try to love the questions themselves. . . ." He goes on to state that "prayer leads us from false certainties to true uncertainties, from an easy support system to a risky surrender, and from the many 'safe' gods to the God whose love has no limits." [9]

Notes

1. Henri Nouwen, *Reaching Out,* Doubleday, 1966, p. 11.
2. Daniel Yankelovitch, "New Rules in American Life: Searching for Self-Fulfillment in a World Turned Upside Down," *Psychology Today,* April 1981.
3. Mary R. Schramm, *Gifts of Grace,* Augsburg, 1982, p. 63.
4. Mary Schramm, p. 62.
5. Oscar Feucht, *Everyone a Minister,* Concordia, 1976, p. 88.
6. Marlene Wilson, *Survival Skills for Managers,* Volunteer Management Associates, 1981, pp. 189-191.
7. Martin Marty, "Simplify Your Life," *Reader's Digest,* March 1980, p. 79.
8. John XXIII, *Journal of a Soul,* Dorothy White, trans., Doubleday, 1980.
9. Nouwen, pp. 11, 90.

Chapter 6

How Do We Become the Scattered Church?

Outreach

Once in a while we experience truly life-changing events. The strange part about these events is how frequently they are, on the surface, ordinary, even mundane happenings. But we know somehow our lives will never be quite the same after that time.

It was just such an event that catapulted me out of my safe, Lutheran pew and into a hurting world. I was reading an article in *The Lutheran Standard* entitled "You're Asking Me What Poverty Is!"[1] In it a woman who had lived in poverty all her life graphically described how being poor felt, tasted, and smelled, and how hopeless she felt as she watched her children trapped in the same web of despair. She ended the article stating "I did not come from another time. I did not come from another place. I am here, now . . . and there are others like me all around you." Something in that woman's story spoke to my deepest being, and the command to be doers of the Word and not hearers only came alive for me. I fell to my knees and prayed the only prayer possible: "I'm available, Lord. Show me what you would have me do."

Since that day, over 15 years ago, I have been on an incredible journey of discovery. The Lord has led me, sometimes gently and sometimes by the scruff of the neck, to people and places in this world that are hurting. This journey began as I served as one of the founders and then as executive director of an agency designed to be the bridge between needs and resources in our community. We handled hundreds of calls for help and found agencies, churches, or individual volunteers who provided what was needed. The agency also served as the connector between volunteers and more than 90 health, youth, senior, and welfare agencies. What an education it was to finally learn about need in the specific versus the abstract!

I now know beyond a shadow of a doubt that we do, indeed, live in a hurting world. The critical question that faces me, and you, and the whole church is, "What do we intend to do about it?" In Mouw's book *Called to Holy Worldliness,* he states:

> Granted that my Christian faith can offer me peace of heart in the midst of the "dog-eat-dog" world, but what does it say *to* the world? . . . If Christianity offers peace to us when we "get away from it all," does it also say something about the "it all" that we have got to get back to? [2]

One of the dilemmas we face in the church today when we speak about outreach or social action is that it is suspect in many circles. It is unfortunate that in some Christian groups evangelism is treated as something very different from social ministry. Congregations are all too often faced with either/or decisions and opt for evangelism.

Much of this sentiment was generated during the turbulent '60s when the call for social action rang through almost every church. Big, important, controversial needs were tearing our nation apart. Fighting in Vietnam, racial injustice, youth rebellion, the drug culture—hardly a family or community was unaffected. We were a nation in agony. So good people marched out to change things and came back disillusioned and confused. People burned with commitment and burned out due to lack of training and preparation. Too often there was little realistic planning. Viable support systems were not in place for those out there "on the line." As Corita Kent observed in her book *Footnotes and Headlines—A Play-Pray Book:* "When groups of humans get bigger—too big for a hug, too many for a single groan . . . then ceremony gets more complex . . . someone's got to order the groceries." [3]

What this points out is that once again the necessary volunteer management systems were not in place—and people thought that if they meant well, things would somehow work out. We need to learn from those experiences! The very systems we have suggested in this book to enable "gathered ministries" also work successfully to enable our "scattered ministries." In both cases, it is a matter of getting our act together in a purposeful way so that we not only know what we want to do, but also are able to do it well. The world needs no less from us!

Richard Neibuhr points out that two misdirected ways the church often has responded to the call for outreach or being the scattered church are:

1. *Worldliness:* the church begins to feel it is more responsible to society for God, than to God for society and becomes just another humanistic movement.

2. *Isolation:* the church responds to God only for itself and rejects not only worldliness but the world.[4]

Our intent in this chapter is to explore some other options.

Why is outreach important?

In my opinion, this chapter is the heart of this book. All of the systems, suggestions, and tools that have been shared are not meant to be used only to make the church a stronger, more effective, and efficient *organization*. (The word *organization* implies an entity with boundaries.) I agree with Niebuhr when he states "The church is not a corporation with limited liability . . . the Christian community must conceive its responsibility in terms of membership in the divine and universal society." [5]

Bonhoeffer defined the world as the sphere of concrete responsibility given to us by and in Jesus Christ, and he believed that Christians are called to the discipleship of Christ in every situation of concrete, everyday life.[6] In other words, if we only concentrate our efforts on making our church structures more effective (and even more humane and caring as I have suggested), we miss the whole point. That is not the end, only a means to the end.

The end we are striving for is to equip Christians to be doers of the Word in all aspects of their lives—in the congregation, in their jobs, in their homes, and in the world. Elizabeth O'Conner states:

> Every inward work requires an outward expression, or it comes to nought. In fact, it may even fracture what we inwardly subscribe to and what we outwardly do. This is why a person's work is always of utmost importance. "Being" and "doing" complete each other, as do "staying" and "going." We cannot choose one above the other without falling into great trouble." [7]

Have you ever thought how much easier it would be for us to make decisions about what to do with our lives if Christ had been a bit more explicit in his directions? If only he'd left us a formula such as:

> 8 hours sleep + 8 hours work + 2 hours eating + 2 hours community service + 1 hour worship and meditation + 1 hour of self-enrichment + 2 hours family activity = one full Christian life!

That would make it all reassuringly simple. All we'd have to do would be to learn the formula. However, in studying Christ's life we find there were times when he meditated day and night; there were times when he missed meals, sleep, and meditation to minister to the needs of others; and there were 40 straight days and nights when he went off by himself into the wilderness to renew himself.

Try as I might, I cannot find a formula. Maybe the reason Christ avoided giving us one was that it might have become a substitute for all the rules and regulations of the Pharisees. We might have tried to make a religion out of the formula and become enslaved by it.

James Burtness warns us of the tyranny of the "oughts and shoulds." He states:

> Any valid description of the Christian life is essentially a gracious offer of a way in which it is possible for a person to live after becoming a Christian, rather than a standard up to which it is necessary to live in order to become a Christian . . . we are condemned to be free. [8]

And Paul Scherer carries that theme forward when he says, "to be free is to plunge into human life up to the elbows, without looking at the price tag or wondering about the payoff, to take inside what's outside, never mind how much it hurts." [9]

Trueblood points out that Christ did leave us the example of how to do this with his three-fold ministry: [10]

- *As Teacher*—He proclaimed God's message in the "here and now." He made it personal and urgent instead of theoretical and historical.
- *As Leader*—He called people to follow him because he needed helpers—and he chose all kinds of people to serve with him.
- *As Healer*—He released people from human suffering wherever he found it.

"Service is not a code of ethics but a way of living." [11] . . . Perhaps that is the formula we are seeking.

What are some opinions regarding service?

While working at the agency I described at the beginning of this chapter, I made it a point to try to involve Boulder's 75 churches in meeting the needs brought to us. I found two common responses. One was ignorance of the need (most congregations simply had no idea there were unmet needs like that in our city); the other was "ignor-ance" (that's knowing about the needs, but doing nothing that really helps to meet them).

I found that often this kind of response was not because the people didn't care enough; it was because they simply did not know any other way to respond. Their churches had not equipped them to be the scattered church in a hurting world.

In the excellent book *Celebration of Discipline,* Richard Foster suggests a number of options for service: [12]

- *The service of hiddenness.* These are the acts of service or gifts of money that are shared anonymously—for the joy of giving. It doesn't matter who gets the credit. If you have read Lloyd Douglas' classic book, *The Magnificent Obsession,* you remember the major theme was that each person was to pass on to someone else the good deeds done for them—but it had to be done anonymously. What a

heartwarming tale that was! Foster says "If all of our serving is before others we will be shallow people indeed." And Dale Carnegie
said "the rare individual who unselfishly tries to serve others has an
enormous advantage. He has little competition!"

• *The service of small things.* These are the seemingly insignifi-
cant day-to-day possibilities that surround each of us in our homes,
communities, and churches. It's "pitching in" and "lending a hand"
—and though it may not seem important, it's these things that create
the climates we live in daily. It either feels good to be there (because we care enough about one another to help however we can)
or it feels cold, lonely, and competitive (everyone for themselves).

Bonhoeffer in *Life Together* talks about the necessity of *active
helpfulness.*

> This means, initially, simple assistance in trifling, external matters.
> There is a multitude of these things wherever people live together.
> Nobody is too good for the meanest service. One who worries about
> the loss of time that such petty, outward acts of helpfulness entail
> is usually taking the importance of his [her] own career too ser-
> iously.[13]

A reaction which most of us probably experience when we contemplate a "scattered ministry" or being in mission goes something
like this: "But I don't want to be a missionary to Africa or some
other foreign country. I want to stay right here!" We say this to
ourselves as we debate the practicality of really turning over our
lives to God. Good grief! Who knows where that could lead us?
Who does know, but God? Paul Scherer points out, "You aren't
likely to be sent out under the will of God to do startling, impossible
things. You are likely to be sent out to do the quiet, unspectacular
things that matter, precisely where you are and with what you
have." [14] Love is simply seeing what needs to be done—and doing it!

• *The service of guarding the reputations of others.* This is the
commitment to stay away from backbiting and gossiping that
so easily can destroy persons—and groups—even in the church.
Have you ever noticed the awful tendency people have to crucify
leaders? I am not talking about the horrifying assassinations of
national leaders we have witnessed in our lifetimes. Instead, I refer

to the all-too-common tendency to slowly kill off people with words and innuendos and accusations. The old playground chant "sticks and stones may break my bones, but words will never hurt me" is simply untrue. Words can kill people—their confidence, self-esteem, initiative and hope, and eventually even their health. Let's serve one another by bringing our concerns and dissatisfactions directly to the persons involved. That means talking *to* them, not *about* them.

• *The service of being served.* We have had the notion that it is more blessed to give than to receive drummed into us so often that we have forgotten it also can be a blessing to be the receiver. One can't be blessed in giving if someone is not willing to receive, and if we feel that *we* must always be the ones giving help, then it says something about our pride. Have you ever had a gift rebuffed or refused? It hurts. When others want to share themselves or their gifts with us, we are unkind if we do anything but accept joyfully and gracefully. "When Jesus began to wash the feet of those He loved, Peter refused. He would never let his Master stoop to such a menial task on his behalf. It sounds like a statement of humility; in reality it was an act of veiled pride. Jesus' service was an affront to Peter's concept of authority. If Peter had been the master he would not have washed feet!" [15]

• *The service of common courtesy.* Perhaps we should call this the service of *uncommon* courtesy. How precious courteous acts have become in our hurried, worried world! When a clerk smiles, when a waitress brings a second cup of coffee, when a driver lets you into the stream of traffic, when a flight attendant holds a cranky baby for a distraught mother, how much nicer the day becomes for all of us! "Please," "thank you," "excuse me"—whatever words or actions will affirm someone else's worth—these are the gifts of service.

• *The service of hospitality.* Peter urges us to "practice hospitality ungrudgingly to one another" (1 Peter 4:9). This means more than just taking turns having one another over for coffee or a meal. It means opening our homes and our lives to others. It is the business of creating *homes,* not *houses,* as places of refuge and renewal for all who enter there, and inviting as many as possible to share your home with you. Our family has changed its attitudes toward entertaining. We do almost no "duty entertaining," i.e., inviting people over for business or social reasons. No matter who we invite, our entertaining is casual and comfortable, with emphasis and time invested in the guests, conversation, and being together instead of in a spotless house, elegant dinner, and faultless serving. It feels so much better, and I think people love it. I know *I* do!

• *The service of listening.* One of the major themes of this book has been helping people tell us who they are. We cannot do that if we don't know how to listen. In Chapter 3, the practices of a good listener were discussed (pages 56-57). It's important to review those elements of good listening and determine how you might personally improve in this incredibly important area of service.

• *The service of sharing the word of life with one another.* I recently heard Lutheran theologian Dale Trautman say that today's Christians are too often like fishermen who camp next to a big lake full of fish, build a fish house, spend all their time debating how to fish, but never get at fishing!

Too often we feel we must play several frightening roles in order to witness to our faith. We must be an *attorney* who can argue the case; a *jury* which decides guilt or innocence; and a *judge* who determines points of law. In reality, all we are to be are *witnesses,* who share what we have experienced, what God has done in *our* lives. To be effective, we need to try simply and honestly to relate three stories:

In *Word and Witness*, a Bible study edited by Foster McCurley Jr. and John Reumann, it is stated:

> Proclaiming the Word of God today is not essentially different from the witnessing of biblical times. This means two things to us. First, God's Word comes to people in the words of other people. Second, proclaiming the Word of God assumes "inspiration," the presence and the work of the Spirit. In spite of human prejudices and errors in judgment, in spite of grammatical peculiarities, nasal tones, and regional dialects, God speaks through human speech to address people. The perfect Word of God can never be separated from the imperfect words of people because that is precisely the way he chooses to meet us. Words can indeed be ambiguous, but they are the least ambiguous means of human communication. So God's Word comes in speeches, sermons, conversations, and dialogue.[16]

And we can enter this type of service with confidence, for we read in Isaiah 55:10-11,

> "For as the rain and snow come
>   down from heaven,
>   and return not thither but water
>   the earth,
> making it bring forth and sprout,
>   giving seed to the sower and bread
>   to the eater,
> so shall my word be that goes forth
>   from my mouth;
>   it shall not return to me empty,
> but it shall accomplish that which I purpose,
>   and prosper in the thing for which I sent it."

• *The service of bearing the burdens of each other.* Henri Nouwen in his book *The Wounded Healer* says that to be a minister in our contemporary society "we must be able to avoid the distance of pity as well as the exclusiveness of sympathy. Compassion is born when we discover in the center of our own existence not only that God is God and man is man, but also that our neighbor really is our fellow man." [17]

The rest of this chapter will deal with this option of service—the whats and hows of helping those in need in our communities. I would hope that instead of choosing one or two of these options of service, we would choose them all—but for the right reason. "Service that is duty-motivated breathes death. Service that flows out of our inward person is life and joy and peace." [18] This is illustrated beautifully in the following poem:

Balloons Belong in Church [19]

I took to church one morning a happy four-year-old child
Holding a bright blue string to which was attached a much loved
    orange balloon with pink stripes . . .
Certainly a thing of beauty.
And if not forever at least a joy for a very important now.
When later the child met me at the door,
Clutching blue string, orange and pink bobbing behind her,
She didn't have to tell me something had gone wrong.
"What's the matter?"
She wouldn't tell me.
"I bet they loved your balloon."
Out it came then, mocking the teacher's voice,
"We don't bring balloons to church."
Then that little four-year-old, her lip a little trembly, asked,
"Why aren't balloons allowed in church? I thought God would like
    balloons."
I celebrate balloons, parades, and chocolate chip cookies,
I celebrate seashells and elephants and lions that roar.
I celebrate roasted marshmallows and chocolate cake and fresh fish.
I celebrate aromas: bread baking, mincemeat, lemons . . .
    I celebrate seeing: bright colors, wheat in a field, tiny wild
        flowers . . .
    I celebrate hearing: waves pounding, the rain's rhythm,
        soft voices . . .
    I celebrate touching: toes in the sand, a kitten's fur, another
        person . . .
    I celebrate the sun that shines slab dab in our faces . . .
    I celebrate snow falling . . . the wondrous quiet of the snow
        falling . . .
    I celebrate the crashing thunder and the brazen lightning . . .
        I celebrate anger at injustice
        I celebrate tears for the mistreated, the hurt, the lonely . . .
I celebrate the community that cares . . . the church . . .
    I celebrate the church.
    I celebrate the times when we in the church made it . . .
    When we answered a cry
    When we held to our warm and well-fed bodies a cold and
        lonely world

I celebrate the times when the Church is the church
  When we are Christians
  When we are living, loving, contributing.
  I celebrate perfect love . . . the cross . . . the Christ
  Loving in spite of . . .
  Giving without reward
  I celebrate life . . . that we may live more abundantly . . .
Where did we get the idea that balloons don't belong in the
    church?
Where did we get the idea that God loves gray and sh-h-h
    and drab and anything will do?
I think it's blasphemy not to appreciate the joy in God's world.
I think it's blasphemy not to bring our joy into His church.
For God so loved the world
That He hung there
Loving the unlovable.
  What beautiful gift cannot be offered unto the Lord?
  Whether it's a balloon or a song or some joy
      that sits within you waiting
      to have the lid taken off?
The Scriptures say there's a time to laugh and a time to weep.
It's not hard to see the reasons for crying in a world where hatred
    is so manifest.
So celebrate!
Bring your balloons and your butterflies, your bouquets of
    flowers . . .
Bring the torches and hold them high!
  Dance your dances, paint your feelings, sing your songs,
      whistle, laugh.
  Life is a celebration, an affirmation of God's love.
  Life is distributing more balloons.
For God so loved the world . . .
Surely that's a cause for Joy.
Surely we should celebrate it!
  Good news! That he should love us that much.
  Where did we ever get the idea that balloons don't belong in
    the church?

Ann Weems

How do we find our scattered ministries?

I suspect we have two major vision problems in the church: (1)
We fail to see the lives of quiet desperation all around us; and

(2) Even if we see the needs, we fail to see what we can do to help.

John Coburn says to each of us:

> What do you bring to minister to other people? You bring your presence. That is all you can bring. That is a great deal because no one else can bring it . . . we are all unique persons . . . and calls to ministry will be as diverse and unique as the people who are called.[20]

I know many Christians who, like myself before I became active at the volunteer referral agency, would like to volunteer in their community but have no idea what is needed or how to go about it. Let me share a few ideas:

Possible volunteer opportunities for individuals

Tutor
Hospital volunteer
Crisis phone counselor
School aide
Little League coach
Red Cross volunteer
Blood donor
Child abuse volunteer
Safe house volunteer
Library aide
Office assistant
Speaker's bureau
Nursing home friend
Crafts teacher
Recreation instructor
Day-care aide
Lap to sit on
Library aide for shut-ins
School crossing guard
Companion to mentally retarded people
Photographer

Meals on Wheels driver
School health aide
Emergency shelter volunteer
Cook for feeding program
Emergency driver
Receptionist
Typist
Computer operator
Newsletter editor
Youth leader (4-H, Scouts, Campfire)
Braille transcriber
Reader for blind people
Red Cross disaster volunteer
Phone aide
Envelope stuffer
Repairperson
Snow shoveler
Translator
Pianist
Wheel chair pusher

These are just a few of the hundreds of opportunities available in most communities. People of all kinds are volunteering to fill these needs. Here are some statistics about volunteerism:

- 41-45% of all volunteers in America are male.
- Retired people are volunteering by the thousands.
- Young people in high school and college are responding eagerly.
- People with disabilities are accomplishing amazing things as givers versus receivers.
- Homemakers are still volunteering (usually in several jobs at once).
- Working people are the fastest growing group of volunteers—they help after working hours and on weekends.
- Families are doing volunteer work together.

To help you locate these volunteer jobs and others, let me make several suggestions:

1. If your church has a volunteer ministries coordinator, he or she should contact the local Voluntary Action Center or Volunteer Bureau if your city has one. (Over 400 communities in the U.S. and Canada now have them, so it's worth checking out.) They would have information on all help-giving agencies and organizations and would have volunteer job descriptions on file for all of them. The church coordinator could then publicize needs in newsletters, bulletins, time and talent surveys and have the information available during member interviews if people express an interest in outreach or social ministry.

2. If your church does not have a volunteer ministries coordinator, visit your city's Voluntary Action Center or Volunteer Bureau yourself. People are there to match you to the appropriate volunteer opportunity.

3. If your community does not have such a center, check the Yellow Pages under Social Service Agencies. Most groups needing help would be listed. Call and ask to speak to the director of volunteers. Watch your local papers for ads and articles highlighting needs for volunteers—then call or visit to get more information.

4. In small towns, usually the schools, churches, Department of Welfare, Red Cross, or library will know where there are needs. Ask them.

The key to a good experience as a volunteer is once again matching your gifts to the appropriate need. There's one "with your name on it." Look for it!

Suggested projects for groups

Often there will be a group within the church that is interested in a social ministry project, or the congregation as a whole may want to undertake one. To locate current needs in your community for group projects, follow the suggestions given for individuals. I also would advise that a task force be set up to personally visit some of the agencies before you decide. Seeing need first-hand tends to heighten commitment and energy. A few suggestions you might want to check out are:

- emergency food/shelter projects
- crisis intervention
- day care for children and/or older adults
- youth center or coffee house
- refugee resettlement program
- renovation of low-cost housing
- neighborhood park renovation
- neighborhood safety program
- after school recreation program
- repair/maintenance of homes of elderly people and people with disabilities
- day-care playground and equipment
- apartment ministries project
- prison jail ministry visitation
- adopt an agency
- emergency needs funds

Several years ago the social action committee of our congregation decided to try a congregation-wide volunteer project—one that was big enough and challenging enough to involve a great many of our members. Our committee members divided up and visited four large agencies in town: Department of Welfare, Mental Health Department, Red Cross, and the Juvenile Justice Center. They interviewed the directors, judge, volunteer directors, etc., and came back to the committee with a report of the needs. After much discussion, the committee recommended to the congregation that Atonement "adopt" the Juvenile Justice Volunteer Program for one year. The judge was delighted, gave a temple talk to the congregation, and the congregation voted to support the project. It was both exciting and frightening. We pledged to the court that our congregation would fill all of the volunteer needs of the Juvenile Probation Department for the year. That meant we had to recruit and schedule our volunteers to cover three programs: nightly jail visitation for both the boys' and girls' jail; weekly pretrial testing of all juveniles to be sentenced; and once a week tutoring at the church for all probationers assigned to that program. Quite an undertaking for a congregation of 600! But our members responded beautifully. People who had been pew-sitters for years came forward; pillars found it a meaningful change of pace; retired persons and professional people loved it. In fact, we not only carried the project through the one year, we kept it for three. (Never underestimate the energy, concern, and commitment that is available.)

There is still another category of social ministry that we need to consider. That is issue-oriented, change-agent efforts. These efforts are often controversial because members may subscribe to different views on any issue. These are the tough ones to address, but as Mouw says:

> It's not enough to say "changed hearts will change society" . . . i.e., racial prejudice. Constitutions have to be rewritten; labor codes have to be changed; jokes and stories must be debunked; self-images need to be repaired; communities have to be rebuilt.[21]

The kinds of issues I'm talking about are things such as low-cost housing, peace, legal aid and justice for elderly people and poor people, women's issues, child and spouse abuse, crime and the justice system, minority rights, Third World concerns, ecology, and unemployment.

William Diehl, in his book *Christianity and Real Life,* talks a great deal about the church's lack of support for people in their Monday through Saturday ministries (in their occupations/vocations, volunteer work, and change-agent roles). In his chapter on "The Ministry of the Change Agent" he makes six observations:[22]

1. The Christian change agent is not out for purposeless change, but focuses on a specific issue that is related to his or her faith (i.e., discrimination is inconsistent with the life and teachings of Christ).

2. Change agent ministries *must* have support groups. They face resistance which brings tension, conflict, and stress. They must not feel alone.

3. The change agent lay minister needs to start where he or she is and grow with events and experience. It's not necessary to be a radical, just be willing to commit your Christian convictions to some form of action.

4. Training must be provided to equip Christian change agents to be effective. Few know how to effect change well.

5. Each change agent must carefully review his or her own ethical position as new tactics are tried.

6. If the change agent is on target with the issue, there will be no "winners" and no "losers" when the change is effected. "Ultimately, all society must benefit from the change."

Many times, in larger group projects or issue-oriented efforts, one group may not be able to tackle the need alone. In many areas of the country consortiums of church and community groups have formed to address needs like emergency shelter and feeding programs, low-cost housing, etc. The needs of the '80s are immense and as governmental dollars are withdrawn from one social program after another, these types of efforts become essential to help meet even the basic needs of people. (A *Time* magazine article stated that as of October 1981 there were 100 million fewer federal dollars per day for social programs and the arts.)

We also have a phenomenon that has been labeled "the new poor"—blue-collar workers who were in steel, auto, and other industries drastically hit by the economy and farmers and small business people who have faced bankruptcy and foreclosures. The needs confront us every time we read a newspaper or turn on a TV or radio. It is impossible for churches to be ignorant of need today, but it is still possible to ignore it.

If your church is attempting a collaborative effort with other concerned groups, it is helpful to be reminded that there are three types of group relationships:

1. *Parasitic.* ($1 + 1 =$ less than 2). This is when turf battles, conflict, and self-interest diffuse the energy of the group. It is a *competitive* style of relationship and very nonproductive.

2. *Symbiotic* ($1 + 1 = 2$). In this case, the groups work *cooperatively.* The result is about equal to what each contributes—a fair exchange of value for value. This works well in times of plenty.

3. *Synergistic* ($1 + 1 = 4$). This is creative *collaboration,* formed on the basis of trust, honesty, open communication, and sharing of resources. It's like quilting—we all have pieces of the answer, but it's not until all the fragments are put together that we get an answer that truly meets the needs better than any one group could do it alone. In my opinion, this is the only relationship that makes sense in times of scarce resources. I hope the church can learn how to work in this way and be a model for others.

As we look at the enormity of the needs for scattered ministry, perhaps we need to reflect on this observation by Henri Nouwen:

> Can we carry the burden of reality? How can we remain open to all human tragedies and aware of the vast ocean of human suffering without becoming mentally paralyzed and depressed? How can we live a healthy and creative life when we are constantly reminded of the fate of the millions who are poor, sick, hungry, and persecuted? . . . Maybe, for the time being, we have to accept the many fluctuations between knowing and not knowing, seeing and not seeing, feeling and not feeling, between days in which the whole world seems like a rose garden and days in which our hearts seem tied to a millstone, between moments of ecstatic joy and moments of gloomy depression, between humble confession that the newspaper holds more than our souls can bear and the realization that it is only through facing up to the reality of our world that we can grow into our own responsibility.[23]

What about agencies wanting to recruit church volunteers?

I have given numerous workshops for community agencies and organizations who have tried, usually unsuccessfully, to tap into the largest army of volunteers in the world—the church. As I listen to them, it often becomes apparent that their lack of success has been as much their fault as the church's.

All too frequently they have been vague in their requests, wishy-washy in their approaches, and in violation of most of the sound volunteer management systems outlined in this book. Questions any organization needs to answer *before* trying to recruit church volunteers (or any other volunteers) are these:

1. Have we designed a plan for our volunteer program this year —with clear goals, objectives, and action plans?

2. Has our paid staff (if we have any) been involved in designing written job descriptions that outline the duties, skills, and the time commitment required for each different type of volunteer involvement?

3. Have we set up interview processes, so each potential volunteer can learn more about our organization and we can learn about their skills, needs, and interests? Is matching the right volunteer to the right job a priority?

4. Have we designed appropriate training opportunities to help our volunteers succeed?

5. Is our staff and volunteer leadership committed to providing enabling supervision and meaningful recognition for all volunteers?

If these steps have not been taken, then it is no wonder people have not responded positively. If they *have* been taken, let me share some other tips for successful recruiting:

• Find out if any of your present volunteers are members of the church you want to reach, and then recruit them to help tell your story.

• Be creative in your appeal. Use slides, client interviews, and graphics as well as verbal information. Tell your story in an interesting and emotionally appealing fashion to as many groups within the church as possible.

• Be specific about your needs and how they as volunteers can help.

• Avoid the "oughts and shoulds" approach.

• Have sign-up sheets or registration forms available after your presentation so people can respond immediately.

• Hold a "Volunteer Opportunity Fair" in collaboration with other agencies who need volunteers and invite all the churches in the area. Make the event informative, creative, and fun!

• Write short, informational "blurbs" about your needs that can

120

be inserted easily in bulletins and newsletters. Direct to the person in charge of those newsletters and bulletins, not the pastor. Make the notices short, snappy, and specific.

• Ask for time on the agenda of the Social Ministries, Social Action, or Social Concerns Committees. Tell your story in person whenever possible.

• Have options. Suggest a variety of individual volunteer jobs and group projects. People like alternatives. And do your homework so your suggestions are appropriate for that group.

• Be enthusiastic!!

Conclusion

We must honestly acknowledge that not all help is helpful nor all motives for service pure—even in the church.

In *Letters to Scattered Pilgrims* we read "many of God's flock go about looking at his world through clouded lenses, using church projects to build up wobbly self-esteem, enlisting dependent people to foster their phony selves, passing off a neurotic need for affection as a loving, caring nature, or the compulsion to be ever busy as priestly concern. Such persons have within themselves all kinds of conflicts which produce dissension in the groups to which they belong. Their vulnerability, excessive demands, expectations, and criticisms make genuine community impossible."[24]

We all have experienced this at some time and know its deadliness. How can we tell about motives, our own or other's? How can we tell the difference between self-righteous service and true service? Richard Foster gives us some guidelines that may help:[25]

Self-righteous service	True service
Enjoys the titanic, "big deal" service—especially if it shows on the ecclesiastical scoreboards.	Doesn't distinguish between large and small service—welcomes both.
Requires external rewards, having others notice and applaud.	Rests content in hiddenness. Doesn't fear the lights and blare of attention but doesn't seek them.

Highly concerned with results and reciprocation. Bitter disappointment if results fall below expectations.	Delights in the service itself, without need to calculate results. Serves enemies as well as friends.
Picks and chooses whom to serve.	Servant of all.
Affected by moods and whims.	Ministers simply because there's a need—the service disciplines feelings rather than vice versa.
Comes through human effort alone—immense energy spent on determining HOW to serve.	Comes from a relationship with the divine. Serves out of "whispered promptings and divine urgings."

We could never live in a time or place where we had more opportunities to live out our faith in meaningful acts of service. The vast array of needs both within the gathered church and in the world is indeed awesome. In fact, it is at times confusing and difficult to know even how to begin to find where we personally could best use our time and gifts.

Elizabeth O'Connor challenges us to study Isaiah 43:19: "Here and now I will do a new thing; this moment it will break from the bud. Can you not perceive it?" (NEB). We must all ask ourselves to name the bud within us that is seeking to break forth. "We can discover the new that God is trying to do through us only by checking within to see where all the sap is building up. That is where the bud is, where God is pushing us out. Within each of us is such a place." [26]

When we discover it, we must simply say yes to it, be aware of those who are "nippers of buds," do the best we can with what we have, and move out in the faith that God will supply the rest. God has promised no less.

" 'Here I am, send me,' is the reply that is full of agony and ecstasy!" [27] It always has been.

Almighty God, you have blessed each of us with unique gifts, and have called us into specific occupations, relationships, and activities using those gifts. Enable us to use our talents to witness to our faith in you and to communicate your love to the people we meet each day. Empower us to be ministers of reconciliation, love, hope, and justice. Keep us steadfast in our commitment to serve actively in your name; through Jesus Christ our Lord. Amen.[28]

Notes

1. "You're Asking Me What Poverty Is!" *The Lutheran Standard*, June 11, 1968, p. 5. The article was copyrighted 1967, by *The Christian Herald* and reprinted by permission.
2. Richard Mouw, *Called to Holy Worldliness*, Fortress Press, 1980, p. 3.
3. Corita Kent, *Footnotes and Headlines: A Play-Pray Book*.
4. Richard Neihbuhr, "The Responsibility of the Church for Society."
5. Neihbuhr.
6. Dietrich Bonhoeffer, *Life Together*, Harper and Row, 1954, p. 8.
7. Elizabeth O'Connor, *Letters to Scattered Pilgrims*, Harper and Row, 1979, p. 108.
8. James Burtness, *Whatever You Do*, Augsburg, 1967, p. 101.
9. Paul Scherer, *Love Is a Spendthrift*, Harper and Row, 1961, p. 138.
10. Elton Trueblood, *Confronting Christ*, Word, 1969.
11. Richard Foster, *Celebration of Discipline*, Harper and Row, 1978, p. 117.
12. Options for service list from pages 117-122 of *Celebration of Discipline: The Path of Spiritual Growth*, by Richard Foster. Copyright © 1978 by Richard J. Foster. By permission of Harper and Row, Publishers, Inc.
13. Bonhoeffer, p. 99.
14. Scherer, p. 52.
15. Foster, p. 119.
16. Foster McCurley Jr. and John Reumann, *Word and Witness*, Division for Parish Services, Lutheran Church in America, 1977, p. 57.
17. Henri Nouwen, *The Wounded Healer*, Doubleday, 1979, p. xv and 41.
18. Foster, p. 122.
19. Ann Weems, "Balloons Belong in Church," *The Church Woman*, Jan. 1978, pp. 4-7. Used by permission.
20. John Coburn, *The Story of Jesus Christ and Your Story*, Forward Movement Publishers, p. 46.
21. Mouw, p. 35.

22. William Diehl, *Christianity and Real Life*, Fortress, 1976, p. 91 ff. Used by permission.
23. Henri Nouwen, *Reaching Out*, Doubleday, 1975, pp. 39, 40.
24. O'Connor, p. 47.
25. Synopsis of some aspects of self-righteous service versus true service from pages 112-113 of *Celebration of Discipline:* The Path of Spiritual Growth, by Richard J. Foster. Copyright © 1978 by Richard J. Foster. By permission of Harper and Row, Publishers, Inc.
26. O'Connor, pp. 109, 111.
27. O'Connor, p. 114.
28. *Occasional Services*, Augsburg, 1982, p. 148.

Appendix A

Levels of Responsibility

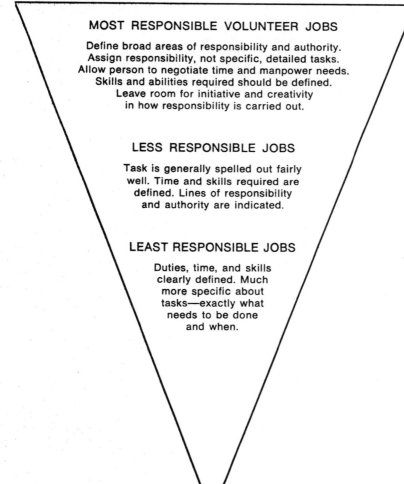

MOST RESPONSIBLE VOLUNTEER JOBS

Define broad areas of responsibility and authority.
Assign responsibility, not specific, detailed tasks.
Allow person to negotiate time and manpower needs.
Skills and abilities required should be defined.
Leave room for initiative and creativity
in how responsibility is carried out.

LESS RESPONSIBLE JOBS

Task is generally spelled out fairly
well. Time and skills required are
defined. Lines of responsibility
and authority are indicated.

LEAST RESPONSIBLE JOBS

Duties, time, and skills
clearly defined. Much
more specific about
tasks—exactly what
needs to be done
and when.

From *The Effective Management of Volunteer Programs* by Marlene Wilson,
Volunteer Management Associates, 1976, p. 108.

Appendix B

A Checklist before Linking a Volunteer

1. Describe the task.
2. Fill out the task design and attach.
3. List where and how to identify the person(s) to involve in the task.
4. What method(s) will be used to ask the person?
5. Once the volunteer is secured and involved, what is the plan of ongoing support?
6. How will you evaluate the volunteer(s)?
7. How will the volunteer be rewarded and recognized?

From "Congregational Workbook," *Volunteerism in the Church* workshops, Division for Life and Mission in the Congregation of the American Lutheran Church, 1980. Developed by Warren Salveson.

Appendix C

Volunteer Questionnaires

Volunteer Network of *(your church)*

Name_____

Address_____

Home phone_____Business phone_____

Age (exact age if under 18) Under 18 _____ 18-20 _____

　　21-30 _____ 31-45 _____ 46-64 _____ 65 and above _____

Occupation_____

Other work experiences_____

_____

Educational experience_____

_____

Leisure activities_____

_____

Prefer to work with:

_____ preschool   _____ seniors
_____ school age   _____ persons with disabilities
_____ teenagers   _____ homebound
_____ young adults   _____ no preference
_____ adults

Transportation: Available _____ Not available _____
                Auto _____ Public transportation _____

Time for volunteering (state hours):
  Monday _____   Tuesday _____   Wednesday _____
  Thursday _____   Friday _____   Saturday _____
  Sunday _____

Skills that I have and would like to share are:_____

_____

_____

Skills I would like to develop are:_____

_____

_____

My hobbies are:_____

_____

_____

I would be interested in knowing about possibilities for service:
_____ in the community, _____ in the district,
_____ in the synod, _____ in church wide agency programs.

My volunteer experience includes: _____

_____

_____

From *Recruiting and Developing Volunteer Leaders* by George Sheiltin and Eleanore Gilstrom, Parish Life Press, Lutheran Church in America, p. 25. Used by permission.

Skills and Service

Witnessing to our faith in Jesus Christ takes many forms in daily life and in the community of believers.

Each year the council and committees of the congregation identify ways in which that ministry can take place. This form indicates the opportunities for members of our congregations to become involved in specific ways with our mission.

Additional information about each of the opportunities for service are available from the volunteer coordinators at the church office.

Our volunteer needs this year

(The following list is a sample of volunteer needs in one congregation. Volunteer services would vary from congregation to congregation and from year to year.)

Please check (√) one or more volunteer services you would be willing to provide this year.

Worship

_____ Usher
_____ Lector
_____ Assisting minister
_____ Altar guild

_____ Senior choir
_____ Junior choir
_____ Worship committee
_____ Acolyte

Learning

Church school teachers for:

_____ Age 3
_____ Grade 5
_____ Youth (12-14)
_____ Youth ministry advisors
_____ Bible study leaders for young adult group
(four Wednesday evenings)
_____ Adult class discussion leader (five weeks)
_____ Catechetical class retreat leader (two overnight retreats)

Vacation church school teachers for:

_____ Nursery—Kindergarten
_____ Grades 1 and 2
_____ Grades 3 and 4
_____ Grades 5 and 6
_____ Music

_____ Assistant director of VCS
_____ Parish education committee

Service

_____ Social ministry committee
_____ Hospital visitation
_____ Homebound visitation
_____ Committee to study congregation's responsibility in the community
_____ Representation on community council for human rights
_____ Please call on me for emergency needs.

List ways you could help:_____

_____

Witness

_____ Evangelism committee
_____ Visitor to inactive members
_____ Visitor to unchurched
_____ Committee on lay ministry
_____ World missions
_____ Interpreter

Support

_____ Stewardship committee
_____ Every Member Response visitor
_____ Leadership development committee
_____ Communications committee
_____ Congregational fellowship nights
         _____ program   _____ refreshments   _____ publicity

This year a special paint/clean-up project will be undertaken. Assistance is needed in:

_____ painting
_____ yard clean-up
_____ carpentry
_____ repairs
_____ housekeeping
_____ gardening
_____ scraping
_____ food preparation

From *Recruiting and Developing Volunteer Leaders* by George Sheiltin and Eleanore Gilstrom, Parish Life Press, Lutheran Church in America, p. 26. Used by permission.

Appendix D

A Variety of Interest Sheets

1. Interests

____ Evangelism	____ Teaching children	____ United Way
____ Stewardship	____ Teacher training	____ Girl Scouts
____ Worship	____ Vacation church school	____ Hospital
____ Education	____ Teaching adults	____ Boy Scouts
____ Property	____ Adult discussion	____ Drug abuse

____ Other (specify) _____

2. Personal preference

____ I would prefer to work alone.
____ I would prefer clear assignments.
____ I prefer challenging new projects.
____ I prefer to be a leader.
____ I prefer to be a follower.
____ I prefer to tackle problems.
____ I prefer to be a part of a group.
____ I prefer to try new things.
____ I prefer an opportunity to meet and
get to know new people.

3. Personal preference

Work alone	_____	Part of a group
Be a leader	_____	Be a follower
Routine tasks	_____	New challenges
See concrete results	_____	Harmonious relationships
Know what's expected	_____	Try new things and design the job

4. Descriptive interest sheet (examples)

____ STEWARDSHIP VISITOR
You will visit people on two nights a month. This will give you an opportunity to make 12 visits over a three-month period. The commitment is for three months. The purpose is to hear where people are at and receive their ideas and concerns; also to inform them of what is happening in the congregation.

____ CARPENTRY

Once a month people with carpentry skills gather at the church and receive assignments for small repair jobs that will take from one to two hours to complete. Young people who would like to work along and learn skills are invited to be a part. The group presently meets on the second Wednesday of the month. Following the work session at about 8:30, the group meets back in the church for sharing and refreshments.

From "Congregational Workbook," *Volunteerism in the Church* workshops, Division for Life and Mission in the Congregation of the American Lutheran Church, 1980. Developed by Warren Salveson.

Appendix E

Storing the Information

Don't lose me

Choose any system you want to retain the information you collect from this process but don't treat it carelessly. A stack of unorganized inventory forms in the file cabinet betrays a lack of respect for the people whose lives they represent. Decide on how the information gathered will be stored and retrieved before you hand out the forms. Some of the systems in use are:

Ring binder

In a small congregation it may be sufficient to collect the forms and keep them neatly in a three-ring binder. Be sure that it is easily accessible in the office for those who have responsibility for locating persons to fill various responsibilities.

Card file

With larger numbers of persons involved, the information needs to be transferred from the inventory and reorganized according to usable categories. In one system there is a card onto which one enters the name of each person who indicated that he or she would be interested in that activity.

Key-sort cards

Available under several different brand names there are cards with preprinted numbers around the edges which can be notched with a simple hand punch. A congregation could establish its own code for these numbers and, with a key-sort needle inserted through a specific number, locate all the persons who had indicated their interest in that activity.

Electronic computers

It is likely that the easiest way (when everything is working) of storing and retrieving such information is in a computer's memory. There will undoubtedly be more congregations discovering the virtues of such a system in the future.

It takes a person

The unanimous opinion we've heard indicates that one person needs to be responsible for maintaining the system. It is very hard for a whole committee to do it.

1. In one congregation there is a volunteer who records the new information as it comes in, keeps the records up to date, brings names to the meetings of the appropriate committees and boards, and is the "steward" of the time and talent system.

2. In another, it is a part of the multitudinous responsibilities of the parish secretary.

3. Congregations employing a person as "Director of Volunteers" make this an integral part of the job description.

From *Sharing Our Gifts* by Art Montgomery, Resource Information Services, Division for Life and Mission in the Congregation of the American Lutheran Church, page 5.

Appendix F

Before and after the Visit

Name of church   Pastor(s) name(s)
Street address
City, State, Zip

Date

Dear _____,

Thank you for our conversation concerning our "Congregational Care" efforts here at our church. I look forward to our visit together.

One of the ongoing challenges of the church as the body of Christ is for its members to know each other as persons—individuals who are unique and important. It would help me to get to know you better if we could talk about some of the following things when we are together:

What would *you* like to see happen in our congregation that would have a real significance for you or your family?

Have you had any disappointments here that you care to share?

Are there ways we, as a church, might better help with the development of your spiritual life? Of your child's? Your parents'? Your friends'?

What have been the *most* meaningful things, *to you,* that you have been involved in here at our church? At another church? In the community? How about the least meaningful?

Tell about your present occupation (and feelings about it if you wish).

What are the things you enjoy doing most in your free time (hobbies, interests, special skills)? Do you feel you have the opportunity to do any of these in the congregation?

Would you prefer more or less or different involvement within the congregation at present?

Are there personal goals and dreams you have that our church might help you realize (things you would like to try, skills you want to develop, interests you would like to pursue)? Feel free to dream a bit. Think of the "if onlys" in your life.

We value greatly your ideas and opinions, and would appreciate your sharing them. Of course, anything shared will be treated with the confidentiality you wish.

You might want to discuss some of these questions with your family ahead of time. That's fine. When I arrive, it would be good to have a place where you and I can visit without disturbing others or being disturbed.

I am looking forward to meeting with you. It is a visit with a beautiful purpose: that we as members of the body of Christ might better be able to know and care for each other, support each other, and celebrate together.

Sincerely,

_____

After My Visit—What Do I Do Now?

What we do with the results of our visits is most important. Some things should be held in confidence, others passed on to appropriate people.

Below are categories under which notes may be taken after the visit. (This paper will not be given to anyone else.)

To enable congregational care ministry

1. Abilities, skills, etc., person may be willing to share:

   a._____tell_____

   b._____tell_____

   c._____tell_____

2. Needs:

   a._____tell_____

   b._____tell_____

   c._____tell_____

3. Helpful facts (job, background, hobbies, experiences, where from, family, education, etc.):

4. Suggestions, ideas:_____

_____

What do I do with the above information?—Call the congregational care coordinator the following day—and go over.

From "Congregational Workbook," *Volunteerism in the Church* workshops, Division for Life and Mission in the Congregation of the American Lutheran Church, 1980. Developed by Marlene Wilson.

Appendix G

Report and Evaluation of a Volunteer Ministry

Name_____Telephone_____

Name of ministry position_____

Term of the position: from_____to_____

1. This ministry position has been satisfying for me because:

134

2. The major frustrations in this ministry position have been:

3. I used the following skills in this ministry position:

4. The training I received for this position included:

5. I felt supported in this position in the following ways:

6. I received the following resources which assisted me in this position:

7. I would have been able to do this ministry better if:

8. The highlights of this ministry for me have been:

9. The major accomplishments which have been achieved through this ministry include:

10. A person following me in this ministry position needs to know:

Please rate each of the following as they enabled you to do this ministry effectively and faithfully by placing an "X" in the appropriate column.

	Outstanding	Average	Inadequate
11. The way in which the position was interpreted and explained to me before I began	_____	_____	_____
12. The training I received for doing the ministry	_____	_____	_____
13. The support I received from the church	_____	_____	_____
14. The challenge and responsibility I felt in doing this ministry	_____	_____	_____
15. The sense of importance the church places on this ministry	_____	_____	_____

The following are about your future volunteer ministries. Please indicate your interest by placing an "X" in the appropriate column.

	Very interested	Somewhat interested	Would like to know more	No interest
16. A new volunteer ministry position				
a. In my church	_____	_____	_____	_____
b. In my community	_____	_____	_____	_____
c. In my denomination	_____	_____	_____	_____
d. In an ecumenical setting	_____	_____	_____	_____

17. Specific volunteer ministry opportunities I would like to explore:

18. Factors in my situation that would influence my next volunteer ministry position:

     Schedule:_____

     Transportation:_____

     Other:_____

19. Additional comments:

Reprinted by permission from "Completing Volunteer Ministries" in the series *The Ministry of Volunteers*. © 1979, Office for Church Life and Leadership, United Church of Christ.

Appendix H

Our Church and Volunteers

Introduction and definitions

The following questionnaire can be a useful tool to stimulate your thinking about your church's volunteer ministry program and to begin to identify parts of the program which might require attention or be a good place to begin when making changes.

The questionnaire may be completed individually, but it probably will be more helpful for a group of leaders to complete it together so that they can work out a consensus on each answer. If people disagree about an issue it indicates that the church needs to clarify its work in this area.

The following questions use *volunteer* to mean a person who does a task without financial compensation and without being forced to do it; *volunteer ministry* to mean the ministry of Christians or the ministry of church members; a *volunteer ministry program* to mean a church's intentional, planned work with its volunteers; and *volunteer ministry position description* to mean written information about the purpose and activities of a volunteer ministry and expectations the church has of the person who does the ministry.

Mission statement of the church

	Yes	No
1. Does your church have a mission statement (a description of its special purpose)? If YES, answer questions 2-6. If NO, skip to 7.	___	___
2. Has the mission statement been reviewed and either affirmed or revised in the last five years?	___	___
3. Is the mission statement regularly referred to as a guide and foundation for the church's program and planning?	___	___
4. Are volunteers in the church familiar with the mission statement?	___	___
5. Do volunteers understand how their volunteer work contributes to the mission of the church?	___	___
6. Does your church regularly establish goals for its life and program?	___	___
7. Who should decide if a mission statement needs to be developed or reviewed, and how it could be done?	___	___

Volunteer ministry position descriptions

1. Is there a list of all volunteer ministry positions in the church?	___	___
2. Generally, do people have a good idea of what is expected of them when they accept a volunteer position?	___	___

	Yes	No

3. Are there written position descriptions for at least 50% of the volunteer ministry positions in the church? _____ _____

4. Are church members aware of what other members are doing as volunteers in the community? _____ _____

5. Do you think at least 25% of the persons from the church who volunteer in community agencies have a written position description? _____ _____

6. Are members of the church aware of what other members are doing as volunteers in the association, conference or other settings of the church? _____ _____

7. Who is, or could be, responsible for identifying volunteer ministry positions and writing position descriptions for them? _____ _____

Identifying volunteers

1. Are members of the nominating committee aware of the gifts, talents, interests and availability of most of the church members? _____ _____

2. Is there any specific method for learning about interests and talents of new members? _____ _____

3. Have most members of the church been given a specific or personal invitation to volunteer to do something that is suited to them? _____ _____

4. Have most church members discussed with a representative of the church what they would like to volunteer to do? _____ _____

5. Is there any record kept which tells what church members would like to do or have been trained to do or have an interest in doing? _____ _____

6. When persons complete a volunteer ministry, do they have an opportunity to explore new ways of volunteering? _____ _____

7. Who is, or could be, responsible for helping church members be aware of the gifts and

138

interests of members so that suitable volunteer ministries can be chosen for them?   _____   _____

Matching volunteers and ministry positions

1. Has every church member been given an opportunity for a specific volunteer ministry?   _____   _____

2. Has the volunteer work been shared by many members rather than by a few who have done most of the work over the years?   _____   _____

3. Has everyone changed, or had an opportunity to change, volunteer positions in the past three years?   _____   _____

4. Has everyone who is participating in a volunteer ministry been given a chance to discuss other possibilities for ministry for which they feel suited?   _____   _____

5. Can you say: "No one ever stopped participating because they simply weren't interested or prepared to do the job"?   _____   _____

6. Is an effort made to make members aware of volunteer ministry opportunities in the community and beyond the local church?   _____   _____

7. Who is, or could be, responsible for deciding what members will be asked to undertake particular volunteer ministries?   _____   _____

Recruiting volunteers

1. Is a face-to-face conversation used for asking persons to serve in volunteer ministries?   _____   _____

2. Are persons being asked to take on a job given a written description of what they are being asked to do?   _____   _____

3. Is everyone who is asked to participate in a volunteer ministry given an accurate picture of how much time and effort it will take to carry it out?   _____   _____

	Yes	No

4. Is everyone who is asked to participate in a volunteer ministry given information about what they need to know in order to do the ministry well?

5. Have all church members been given a choice in volunteer ministry positions?

6. Are persons told why they were chosen to be asked to undertake a particular volunteer ministry?

7. Who is, or could be, responsible for recruiting members for ministry positions within your church?

Training volunteers

1. Before people take on new positions do they participate in an orientation session?

2. Is there some way for persons who have completed a position to pass on helpful information to the persons who take over their positions?

3. Are learning opportunities provided for members as they carry out a volunteer ministry?

4. Does your church sponsor retreats, Bible study or specific courses designed to help volunteers develop new skills and knowledge?

5. Does your church pay for members to attend training sessions outside the church?

6. Are all ministry positions currently filled by people adequately trained to do them?

7. Within the church, who is, or could be, responsible for a training program for volunteers?

Supporting volunteers

1. Do all volunteers receive orientation and training for their tasks so that they can go about them with confidence and work effectively?

140

	Yes	No

2. Do all volunteers know there is someone available to assist and encourage them? _____ _____

3. Generally, are church members aware of persons doing volunteer ministry on their behalf in the community and beyond the local church? _____ _____

4. Are volunteers recognized and thanked by the church for their services? _____ _____

5. Do volunteers have adequate resources to carry out their work? _____ _____

6. Are records kept of the volunteer services of each member? _____ _____

7. Who is, or could be, responsible for supporting volunteers? _____ _____

Completing a volunteer ministry

1. When people undertake a volunteer ministry do they know how long it will last? _____ _____

2. Is it impossible to take on a volunteer position in the church "for life" without renewing the commitment from time to time? _____ _____

3. Does the church have a way of saying thanks to people who have volunteered on its behalf? _____ _____

4. When a volunteer ministry is completed, does the volunteer have an opportunity to discuss how it went, what was accomplished, what was learned and what the frustrations were? _____ _____

5. Do continuing members of church organizations have an opportunity to say "good-bye" to completing members at the end of their terms? _____ _____

6. Are people recognized by the church or its organizations when they complete volunteer ministries? _____ _____

7. Who is, or could be, responsible for developing ways to recognize and deal with persons who are completing a volunteer ministry? _____ _____

141

	Yes	No

Evaluating the volunteer ministry

1. Is there a designated group of persons whose responsibility is to evaluate the church's volunteer ministry program? _____ _____

2. Have volunteers been given an opportunity to express their feelings about their work and to suggest changes in the church's volunteer ministry program? _____ _____

3. Has there been at least one significant change in the volunteer ministry program during the past year? _____ _____

4. Are there individuals or groups working on each area of the church's volunteer ministry program covered by this questionnaire? _____ _____

5. Is evaluation seen by the church as a way to improve and work for greater excellence rather than as criticism? _____ _____

6. Have you understood the concepts and terms used in this questionnaire? _____ _____

7. Who is, or could be, responsible for evaluating your church's volunteer ministry program? _____ _____

Reprinted by permission from "The Church and Its Volunteers" in the series *The Ministry of Volunteers* © 1979, Office of Church Life and Leadership, United Church of Christ.

Appendix I

Sample Job Descriptions

1. Job title   Coordinator of Volunteer Ministries

Responsible to   Senior pastor as staff supervisor; volunteer ministries task force as advisors

Job description

Responsible for staffing the volunteer ministries project, including:
1. Defining volunteer needs of congregation; seeing that descriptions of all opportunities are written.

2. Coordinating one-to-one visits with all confirmed members, including recruiting and training interviewers and scheduling interviews.
3. Developing and maintaining appropriate record/retrieval systems for needs, interests, and skills of our members.
4. Coordinating the matching of skills, interests, and needs.
5. Following up on volunteer placements.
6. Initiating appropriate training for volunteers.
7. Facilitating recognition for volunteers.
8. Working closely with all appropriate council committees.

Time required   20 hours per week for one year; longer if mutually agreeable.

In-service training provided   Volunteer management training courses; consultation with task force members and community volunteer coordinators.

Qualifications and special skills   Honest caring for people; organizational skills; motivator and enabler.

Comments   This is a pivotal position on the ministerial staff of the church and will involve weekly meetings with the rest of the church staff. The volunteer ministries task force will provide guidance, assistance, and support.

---

2. Job description for volunteer coordinator

Purpose
The purpose of this position shall be to provide assistance and organization in the volunteer work within the congregation.

Responsibilities
1. Keep up-to-date records concerning volunteer services within the congregation.
   Records may include: information on members' occupations, skills, hobbies; past and present involvement of members in church and community activities.

2. Coordinate annual time and talent survey.
   This will include adequate follow-up on those who fail to fill out time and talent sheets.

3. After time and talent survey is completed, coordinator shall tabulate and provide the various boards, committees, and organizations with information pertinent to their work.
4. Serve as resource person when special needs for volunteer service arise.
5. Find ways of encouraging more involvement of the uninvolved—provide committees and organizations with names of people who are not yet involved who should be considered and encouraged.

Organization
1. Coordinator may recruit people to help fulfill responsibilities of this office.
2. Coordinator shall prepare a report for inclusion in annual printed report of congregation.
3. Coordinator shall be appointed by the board of deacons.
4. Coordinator shall be responsible to the board of deacons.
5. Coordinator shall work closely with parish secretary concerning records and supplies.

Promotion
Coordinator may write occasional articles for the congregation's monthly paper to encourage the cause of volunteer service and to note special needs in congregation and community.

---

3. Job description   Coordinator of Human Resources

Responsible to   The pastor

Responsibilities
1. Develop and administer an in-house volunteer program including recruitment, interviewing, and matching of people, skills, and tasks.
2. Sensitize and train church staff and programmatic leadership to effectively utilize, train, and work with volunteers.
3. Direct and coordinate use of the annual time and talent sheets.
4. Act as advocate for volunteers and promote appreciation for volunteers within congregational life and mission.
5. Attend staff meetings at least monthly and appropriate committee meetings when requested.
6. Attend at least one workshop annually in area of volunteerism, keep current with publications in the field, and serve as liaison with community volunteer activities.
7. Serve as "broker" for people in crisis situations with capacity to use church and community resources for referral.

4. Job title   Coordinator of Volunteer Ministries

Responsible to   Task Force on Volunteer Ministries

Job description

1. Be a listener to parish needs.
2. Encourage an awareness and commitment to lay ministry.
3. Assist in describing volunteer jobs.
4. Encourage the use of sound recruitment procedures.
5. Assist in matching people with skills and interests to the jobs that need to be done.
6. Develop and maintain a volunteer filing system.
7. Assist in developing the leadership program.
8. Encourage the support and recognition of volunteers.
9. Be a member of volunteer task force.

Length of service   One year contract, renewable.

In-service training provided   As requested.

Qualifications and special skills

1. Be committed to the mission of the church in the congregation.
2. Have the ability to get along with people and win their cooperation.
3. Have the ability to organize.
4. Have experience as a volunteer.
5. Have perseverance, enthusiasm, dedication, and a sense of humor.

Appendix J

Are You—or Can You Be—a Creative Leader/Manager?

A study of creative executives identified 25 traits they had in common. If we are interested in becoming creative leaders/managers, we would do well to evaluate ourselves against this yardstick of characteristics to see:

1) Am I satisfied with the extent to which I have developed each trait?
2) If not, do I want to work to develop this trait?
3) If I want to work to develop a trait, what are some concrete steps I might take? (Creativity does not just happen without effort and intentionality!)

Below are 25 qualities of a creative leader. Answer the questions and then pair off with one other person and act as consultants to each other. Focus on the "Want to Develop" column where either of you has checked it, and talk about ways to work at improving this skill or quality.

Choose two or three action steps you will take, beginning tomorrow, to start moving along toward becoming a more creative leader.

A creativity checklist

	Yes	No	Want to develop
1. Have I maintained a youthful curiosity about most things?	—	—	——
2. Am I able to remain relatively open to new, unusual, or venturesome ideas?	—	—	——
3. Am I sensitive to problems and eager to find fresh approaches to solving them?	—	—	——
4. Do I dare to transcend accepted patterns of thinking and stick to convictions in the face of possible discouragement or censure?	—	—	——
5. Am I willing to give up immediate gain, comfort, or success to reach long-range goals?	—	—	——
6. Do I have a greater than average amount of energy?	—	—	——
7. Do I have many hobbies, skills, and interests?	—	—	——
8. Am I comfortable toying with ideas vs. needing to find quick solutions?	—	—	——
9. Can I tolerate ambiguity and juggle many possibilities simultaneously (even though they may seem conflicting or even contradictory)?	—	—	——
10. Am I able to choose the more fundamental and reject the superfluous?	—	—	——
11. Do I possess a "creative memory" which rearranges, prunes, discards, relates, and refines data and ideas?	—	—	——
12. Do I allow incubation time for ideas so I can contemplate, reflect, and let them gel?	—	—	——
13. Am I conscious of my own personal rhythm of output? (Am I creative in the morning, late night, outside, sitting at a desk?)	—	—	——
14. Do I persevere in spite of obstacles and opposition?	—	—	——
15. Can I evaluate my own ideas objectively after I have elaborated them?	—	—	——
16. Do I feel I (and those who work with me) have untapped potentials?	—	—	——

	Yes	No	Want to develop
17. Do I have a lot of initiative?	—	—	——
18. Do I eagerly ask questions?	—	—	——
19. Do I compete with myself rather than others?	—	—	——
20. Am I willing to listen to every suggestion but judge situations for myself?	—	—	——
21. Am I open and direct with people, respecting their rights?	—	—	——
22. Am I often irritated by the status quo and refuse to be bound by habit or norms?	—	—	——
23. Do I like ventures involving calculated risks?	—	—	——
24. Do I avoid making excuses for mistakes and keep from blaming others?	—	—	——
25. Am I willing to stand alone when integrity demands it?	—	—	——

Action steps I will take, beginning tomorrow, to develop some of the traits of a more creative leader:

1. _____

2. _____

3. _____

Reprinted from *Survival Skills for Managers* by Marlene Wilson, Volunteer Management Associates, 1981. Developed by Marlene Wilson from the article "Are You a Creative Executive?" by Eugene Roudsepp, Management Review, February 1978.

Appendix K

Blocks to Creativity

Block	Definition
1. Fear of failure	Drawing back; not taking risks; settling for less in order to avoid the possible pain or shame of failing.
2. Reluctance to play	Literal, overly serious problem-solving style; not "playing around" with stuff. Fear of seeming foolish or silly by experimenting with the unusual.

3. Resource myopia	Failure to see one's own strengths; lack of appreciation for resources in one's environment—people and things.
4. Overcertainty	Rigidity of problem-solving responses; stereotyped reactions; persistence in behavior that is no longer functional; not checking out one's assumptions.
5. Frustration avoidance	Giving up too soon when faced with obstacles; avoidance of the pain or discomfort that is often associated with change or novel solutions to problems.
6. Custom-bound	Overemphasis on traditional ways of doing things; too much reverence for the past; tendency to conform when it is not necessary or useful.
7. Impoverished fantasy life	Mistrusting, ignoring, or demeaning the inner images and visualizations of self and others; overvaluing the so-called objective, real world; lack of "imagination" in the sense of "let's pretend" or "what if."
8. Fear of the unknown	Avoidance of situations which lack clarity or which have unknown probability of succeeding; overweighting what is not known versus what is known; a need to know the future before going forward.
9. Need for balance	Inability to tolerate disorder, confusion or ambiguity; dislike of complexity; excessive need for balance, order, symmetry.
10. Reluctance to exert influence	Fear of seeming too aggressive or pushy in influencing others; hesitancy to stand up for what one believes; ineffectiveness in making oneself heard.
11. Reluctance to let go	Trying too hard to push through solutions to problems; inability to let things incubate, or let things happen naturally; lack of trust in human capacities.

12. Impoverished emotional life	Failure to appreciate the motivational power of emotion; using energy in holding back spontaneous expressions; lack of awareness of the importance of feelings in achieving commitment to individual and group effort.
13. Unintegrated yin-yang	Not making sufficient use of contrasting ways of getting at the essence of things; polarizing things into opposites, rather than knowing how to integrate the best of both sides; lacking unified perception of the wholeness in the universe.
14. Sensory dullness	Not adequately using one's primary senses as a way of knowing; making only partial contact with self and environment; atrophy of capacities to explore; poor sensitivity.

Appendix L

Description of Volunteer Opportunities

Job title:_____

Responsible to:_____

Job description:_____

_____

Time required (Specify both approximate hours per month and the term of the job):_____

In-service training provided:_____

_____

Qualifications and special skills:_____

_____

(To help in defining the job, review the chart in Appendix A, p. 125, to determine which level job it is.)

Appendix M

Resistance to Change

Perhaps we might gain a bit of insight into this strange and frustrating situation by looking at eight areas of change where resistance usually occurs in any situation. *Remember—the essence of innovation is change.*

1. Changes that are perceived to *lower status or prestige.*
2. Changes that *cause fear.*
3. Changes that *affect job content and/or pay.*
4. Changes that *reduce authority or freedom of acting.*
5. Changes that *disrupt established work routines.*
6. Changes that *rearrange formal and informal group relationships.*
7. Changes that are *forced without explanation or employee participation.*
8. Changes that are resisted because of *mental and/or physical lethargy.*

How might this speak to volunteer programs? (Discussion in triads.)

Hodge and Johnson, *Management and Organization Behavior,* Wiley and Son, 1970.

Appendix N

Characteristics of a Servant/Leader

1. The servant/leader is servant first, to whom followers grant leadership after they have been well served.
2. The servant/leader's openness to inspiration and insight provides vision and direction.
3. Invites others to go along and trusts them to do so.
4. Always knows and can articulate the bigger goal, the vision, the dream, which excites followers' imagination and sustains their spirits.
5. Is an intent listener, knowing that genuine listening both builds strength in others and provides information for problem solving.
6. Can take the abstract idea and facilitate the hearer's "leap of imagination" drawn from the hearer's own personal experience so it all makes sense.
7. Can systematically neglect the less important while choosing to do the more important.
8. Knows when to withdraw and regroup or take time for reorientation.
9. Accepts person unqualifiedly; never rejects person, but may reject performance.

10. Empathizes with others by being able to get into their shoes. Genuine interest in and affection for the followers.
11. Can tolerate imperfection in self and others.
12. Uses own intuitive insight to bridge the gap in available information to make decisions, and has good record of right decisions. Knows when to decide.
13. Possesses foresight about what is going to happen when in the future, and the ethical resolve to act on that while action is still possible.
14. Thorough preparation for a situation, with faith that if one releases the analytical thought processes, a solution will appear from the creative deeps.
15. Ability to be on two levels of consciousness always: (1) in the real world, involved and responsible; and (2) detached and standing outside the real world, seeing it in the long sweep of history and future.
16. Is aware of life and the environment in a way that gives own intuitive computers a lot of data to work with.
17. Believes that in the stress of real life one can compose oneself in a way that permits the creative process to provide answers. An inner serenity.
18. Persuasion, rather than coercion, convinces one to change.
19. Knows who he or she is able to be own person, choosing own role.
20. Perseverance—one step at a time toward the goal in spite of frustrations.
21. Can conceptualize change and instill the spirit to work for change in those who have to accomplish the change.
22. Can wait until the group of people can define their own need for wholeness or healing.
23. The servant/leader is motivated for work by own need for wholeness or healing.
24. Believes that only in community is an individual healed and made whole.
25. Views institutions as necessary to our survival, but believes they must become people-building institutions, not people-destroying institutions.
26. Understands that those leaders (trustees) who stand outside the institution but who are charged with seeing that the institution is making progress toward its goals are the very leaders who have the greatest potential for raising the quality of the whole society. They need to be servant/leaders.
27. Recognizes coercive power because he/she has been exposed to it and knows its bitterness. He or she could use it but chooses not to because it diminishes the followers.
28. Knows that change must start inside oneself, not "out there"; that all problems are inside oneself, not "out there."

29. Recognizes "the enemy" as strong natural servants who have the potential to lead, but do not lead, or who choose to follow a nonservant.
30. Recognizes that preparation to lead must become a top priority.

Summarized from *The Servant as Leader* by Robert K. Greenleaf, Windy Row Press. Used by permission.

Appendix O

Personal Plan of Action Worksheet

1. I want to achieve the following goals to help me become more of an enabler to others:

2. What are some of the positive things that might happen if I reach this goal?

3. What are my chances for success?   Why do I feel this way?

   _____ Very good   _____

   _____ Good   _____

   _____ Fair   _____

   _____ Poor   _____

   _____ Very poor   _____

4. What are some of the negative things that might happen if I reach this goal?

5. What could keep me from reaching this goal?

   _____ I don't really have the skills, ability, and/or knowledge needed.

   _____ I don't want it badly enough to really work for it.

   _____ I'm afraid that I might fail.

   _____ I'm afraid of what others might think.

   _____ Others don't want me to reach this goal.

   _____ This goal is really too difficult to ever accomplish.

   Some other reasons might be:

6. What are some things I could do so the above things don't pre-vent me from reaching my goal?

7. Do I still want to try to reach this goal?

_____ Yes

_____ No

_____ Undecided

8. Who can help me?

Name: _____

Kind of help: _____

_____

9. What are some first steps I could take to reach this goal?

10. What else must I do if I am really to succeed?

11. Am I going to take the above steps?

_____ Yes

_____ No

_____ Still undecided

12. If my answer to No. 11 is Yes, I make the following self-contract:

Self-contract

I, _____, have decided to try to achieve the

goal of _____. The first step I will take to reach

this goal will be to _____ by _____. My target

date for reaching this goal is _____.

Date _____   Signed _____

Witnessed by _____

Appendix P

Stress Management: A Necessary Survival Tool for Today's Professional

by Marlene Wilson, author of *Survival Skills for Managers* and *The Effective Management of Volunteer Programs*

When did you last have one of those stressful days — the kind that proves Murphy's law about everything going wrong that possibly could:

—The alarm didn't go off and you missed your 8:30 staff meeting.
—The boss turned down that proposal you submitted three weeks ago.
—The secretary was out with a cold so you answered phones all day.
—You got stuck in a one-hour traffic jam on the way home from work.

As the pressure mounts, so does your blood pressure and soon your head aches or your stomach hurts, you begin snapping at everyone (including strangers), your heart pounds and you find yourself either becoming more aggressive or withdrawing into yourself.

What are you experiencing is a stress attack, and it is one of the most common phenomena in today's world of work. According to management expert Karl Albrecht, stress-related illness costs industry over 150 billion dollars a year. It has become known as the "quiet killer," as it contributes to most of the major health problems (i.e., heart disease, hypertension, ulcers, cancer).

It is therefore essential that as a professional in today's world, you not only understand stress, but learn to manage it effectively if you are to survive in a healthy, productive, and successful manner. Your very life may depend on it!

Let's examine that theoretical hectic set of events we just listed. There are three components of stress in each of them.

1. The stressor—that event or incident in the environment that arouses stress.

2. Your perception of that stressor (how will it affect you).

3. Your reaction or physical and emotional response to the stressor based on that perception.

This information explains why some people view a seemingly stressful incident so much more calmly than others. Let's take the traffic jam for instance. One person impatiently views it as an intrusion on his freedom of movement and a maddening inconvenience, while the person in the next car may regard it as a chance to listen to a favorite tape or unwind before reentering his or her life with the family. It's the same traffic jam—but both the perceptions and reactions are very different. Therefore, it is stress-inducing to one and stress-reducing to the other.

What this points out is that in coping with stress, we have three options:

1. Remove ourselves from the situation or stressor.
2. Reengineer the situation so it is no longer stressful.
3. Teach ourselves to react differently (change our attitudes) regarding things we find stressful that we cannot change or leave.

Research has shown that it is prolonged, unrelieved stress that is the most debilitating, so those are the situations to work on first. Two frequent responses to stress are either anger or fear and they evoke different reactions:

Anger—fight

Fear—flight

Both responses involve the entire body. The stress response pumps the necessary adrenalin and blood throughout our system to help us mobilize for action. When we stay in a stressful situation too long, we end up "stewing in our own juices," and this can have serious consequences to our health and well-being.

Dr. Donald Tubesing, a well-known author and lecturer on stress management, sounds a hopeful note. He states that most people handle 98 percent of potentially stressful situations successfully. The other 2 percent are what cause the problem. He and other experts remind us that not all stress is bad, as it is often what provides the excitement and zest that counteracts boredom and stagnation. The key is to find your appropriate and healthy stress level and to choose which stresses to keep and which to shed.

Tubesing also notes that this sorting-out process can be facilitated by asking yourself these three questions:

1. Does a threat exist?
2. Is it worth a fight?
3. If I fight will it make a difference?

By answering these questions, it will help you keep from "spending $10 worth of adrenalin on a 10 cent problem." The goal is to try to learn to expend the appropriate amount of energy on problems or stressors based on their long-term importance to you. If you overreact to small things (like traffic jams and lost socks), you will use up your stress energy inappropriately.

One of the most seductive temptations for human services professionals is to try to be all things to all people. (This is sometimes referred to as the "Messiah Complex.") It is what leads to longer and longer hours, more and more projects, weekend and evening commitments, and eventual burnout. It often looks easier, quicker, and more effective to do things yourself rather than going through the time and effort to recruit, train, and supervise volunteers to help you help your clients. (Besides, it's kind of nice to feel you have climbed on that pedestal called "indispensable." Remember—the only way to get off a pedestal is down and it behooves you to climb down before you fall off!)

It is important to remember a large part of your job is to be a manager: someone who works with and through others to accomplish organizational goals. And how those "others" feel about working with you has:

a tremendous impact on both the quality and quantity of work they will do . . . which has

a tremendous impact on your own perceptions of your effectiveness as a manager . . . which has

a tremendous impact on both your own stress level and that of your subordinates . . . which has

a tremendous impact on your health and peace of mind.

In my book *Survival Skills for Managers* I list several suggestions to help manage the stress in your life:

1. Clarify your value system to be sure that the greatest time and energy you are expending are going toward those things of greatest value to you.

2. Take good care of yourself physically through exercise and good nutrition.

3. Create and use personal support systems.

4. Learn to let go of past resentments, toxic relationships, and bad health habits.

5. Seek variety and a well-rounded personality—avoid being a one-dimensional workaholic.

6. Maintain optimism and keep some optimists around you.

7. Try to make the workplace and work itself more enjoyable.

8. Don't let small things become a hassle.

9. Take responsibility for yourself:
    a) take action today to change what needs to be changed;
    b) develop creativity and flexibility; and
    c) have faith that things can be different.

Most of the effective managers I have known have been, first of all, effective as persons. By that I mean they are well-rounded, involved, enthusiastic lifelong learners who always see themselves on a "journey of becoming."